中國夢‧廣東故事
——開放的廣東

作者　劉曉星　LIU XIAOXING

The China Dream :
Guangdong Story -
Openness

Editors: Zeng Yuhan, Liao Zhicong

Published by Guangdong People's Publishing House Ltd., China

www.gdpph.com

First published 2017

Printed in the People's Republic of China

The China Dream: Guangdong Story-Openness/ Liu Xiaoxing and translated by Yang Chengxi

ISBN 978-7-218-11889-5 (paperback, 1st edition)

Preface

Located in southern China, Guangdong Province is the first region in China to implement the reform and opening up, and it is also one of the most affluent areas nationwide. The Pearl River, China's third largest river, runs across the whole province. The Pearl River Delta is an alluvial plain flushed by the Pearl River. After nearly 40 years of rapid development, it has already become one of the most important city groups of China. The Hong Kong Special Administrative Region, and the Macao Special Administrative Region adjoin to Guangdong Province. With the natural geographical relations and the same cultural background, they constitute China's unique Guangdong-Hong Kong-Macao Greater Bay Area—a world-class vigorous economic and cultural area.

For nearly 40 years of rapid development, Guangdong has been playing a leading role in innovation, spurring the rapid development of new growth drivers. There are many rapidly grown-up enterprises in Guangdong, such as Huawei, Tencent, and UMi, which have become important engines of Guangdong's new economy development. Huawei and Tencent are now widely known in China. We try to approach such enterprises and their employees, to find the "secret" of the most innovative and cutting-edge development in Guangdong.

Guangdong has been the most dynamic foreign trade area in China since ancient times. And Guangzhou has been a commercial city through the ages, as well as an important interconnecting city alongside the "Maritime Silk Road". Foreigners from all over the world travel across major cities in Guangdong everyday, sightseeing, attending business meetings, studying or visiting friends. In Guangzhou, there are a large number of foreigners from Europe, America, Southeast Asia, the Middle East, Africa and other places, doing business here everyday. They ship back clothing, fabric, seafood, electrical appliances or glasses; foreign trade is booming. In the Shenzhen Special Economic Zone ports, people and vehicles travelling between Hong Kong and Shenzhen are always lined up. Foreigners living here for many years gradually adopt and merge into customs and culture of Guangdong, and regard Guangdong as their "second home". Meanwhile, tens of millions of workers from other provinces live in Guangdong, especially in the Pearl River Delta, where they work in factories, earn money to support their families, and try to realize their own dreams and ambitions. Whether foreigners or migrant workers, they are all practitioners, promoters and witnesses of Guangdong's reform and opening up. We conduct close observation of their work and life to record their up and downs.

Ten years ago, the per capita income in the Pearl River Delta had already reached the level of that of moderately developed countries, and it is moving towards high-income phase. But the embarrassment is that in the eastern, western and northern parts of Guangdong Province, there are still large number of underdeveloped rural areas, and some places are even in extreme poverty, which distresses successive provincial governments. The government is determined to carry out large-scale " poverty alleviation" action, and vows to lift all peasants of impoverished areas out of poverty in three years, and promote common prosperity in these parts of Guangdong like the Pearl River Delta.

As the most populated, dynamic, and developed province that has been spearheading reform and opening up, recent practices in Guangdong are full of strength and sweetness. We go into it, and hope to find and record those breathtaking, touching and impressive stories of the development in Guangdong these years. Those people and those stories constitute a glaring part in the glittering development of the new era in Guangdong.

Through these stories, you can see diligence and endeavors of Guangdong people in the process of modernization. Through the perspective of Guangdong, you can see great efforts of Chinese people in realizing the China dream of the great rejuvenation of the Chinese nation.

總序

　　廣東省位於中國南部，是中國最早實行改革開放的區域，也是目前中國最富庶的地區之一。中國的第三大河流珠江穿越廣東省全境，由珠江沖積而成的珠江三角洲在經過近四十年迅速發展後，已經成為中國最重要的城市群之一。香港特別行政區、澳門特別行政區與廣東省毗鄰，天然的地緣和一脈相承的人文情緣，構成了中國獨有的粵港澳大灣區——一個世界級活躍的經濟人文區域。

　　和中國其他地區一樣，在經過長達近四十年的高速發展之後，廣東面臨產業轉型升級轉變發展動能的重任，創新驅動成為推動此輪變革的重要抓手。廣東省內有許多近年來快速成長起來的新型企業，比如華為、騰訊、有米科技，它們成為廣東新經濟發展的重要引擎。華為和騰訊，以及它們的「老闆」任正非和馬化騰，在中國幾乎家喻戶曉。我們試圖走近這樣的企業及其員工，找到廣東創新驅動最前沿的發展「密碼」。

　　廣東自古以來是中國對外商貿最活躍的地區，廣州是千年商都，是「海上絲綢之路」重要的節點城市。來自世界各地的外國人每天往來於廣東省內各大城市，他們或旅遊觀光，或商務會議，或求學訪友。在廣州，每天大量來自歐美、東南亞、中東和非洲等地的外國人在這裡做生意，他們把這裡的服裝、布匹、海產品、電器或者眼鏡託運回國，外貿做得紅紅火火。在深圳經濟特區口岸，進出香港和深圳的車輛、人流常常排成長龍。長年生活在這裡的外國人，在生活習俗和文化上逐漸接受並慢慢融入廣東，廣東成為他們的「第二故鄉」。與此同時，更多的數千萬計的來自中國內地的普通勞工常年生活在廣東尤其是珠江三角洲地區，他們在工廠裡「打工」，憑藉「打工」掙下的錢養家餬口，並試圖實現自己的人生夢想。無論是外國人還是農民工，他們都是廣東改革開放的實踐者、推動者和見證者。我們近距離觀察他們的工作和生活，記錄他們的喜怒哀樂。

珠江三角洲地區早在十年前人均收入便已達到中等發達國家水平，正邁向高收入階段。但令人尷尬的是，在廣東省的東、西、北部仍有大片生活並不富裕的農村，一些地方甚至還處於貧困狀態，這讓廣東省歷屆政府頗感頭痛。政府下決心開展大規模的「扶貧」行動，並發誓要在三年後讓所有貧困地區的農民擺脫貧困，力促粵東西北地區與珠江三角洲地區走向共同富裕。

作為人口最多、經濟最活躍、總量最大、地處改革開放前沿的省份，廣東近年的實踐既具有力量又讓人感到溫馨。我們深入其中，希望通過我們去發現去記錄，在廣東發展這些年中，那些或動人心魄或充滿溫情或飽含人性的故事。那些人，那些事，終將構成廣東新時期史詩般發展歷程中炫目的一環。

通過這些故事，人們可以看見，在現代化進程中廣東人的奮發圖景；透過廣東，可以看見中國人民為實現中華民族偉大復興的中國夢的奮鬥歷程。

Contents

Since I am Here, I am not Leaving

目錄

來了，就不想離開

Century-aged Brand
"Jing Hua Fish Ball"

Dainty Fish Ball Descending through Five Generations

One winter back in the 1980s, it was not yet four o'clock in the morning and the sun has not yet risen. Liang Zhibo raced to the dock with heavy laden eyelids to check the freshness of the fish on the fishing boats. What a cold day for fishing! Yet, it was widely considered that fish in both autumn and winter are the freshest and most tender in texture for the finest fish balls. At that time, there was no ice nor cold storage techniques. Once the fishing boats were pulled in to the shore, the fish had to be bought in and made into fish balls by the craftsmen immediately. Liang Zhibo rolled up his sleeves, "Let's get started." The first and key step is to scrape the flesh from the bones of the fish. Being adept at the process, Liang handled the knife skillfully. Before we noticed the fall of the knife, the fish's head, skin, bones and tail were gone. Then the flesh was ground into a thick paste and was put into special handmade casks with special sauce. The second crucial step is to pound the flesh till it reaches the right consistency. The trick to the fish balls' soft, springy texture is slapping and pounding the fish paste over and over until it turns smooth and glossy. It usually took thousands of times of lifting and slapping before the paste was ready for shaping into balls. Both the slapping strength and the time are of crucial importance. Otherwise, the fish paste would turn either loosening and grainy or hard in texture, losing the crunchy feel to it. After that, Liang Zhibo grabbed the fish paste in between the crook of his thumb and index finger and squeezed the balls out into cold water. When the fish balls congealed, they are ready to be dropped into the pot to finish cooking. As he waited, a smell of fresh fragrance penetrated the room and went into his nose... It's thrilling and animating to watch the cooked fish balls pop up and down in the slotted spoon, radiating a tasty smell.

One morning in December 2016, Liang Shaozhong, Liang Zhibo's son, drove to the food factory after cleaning up and getting dressed. He was going to inspect and supervise the work of the workers and boost their morale. Twenty minutes later, Liang Shaozhong arrived at the factory. He looked up at the banner hanging above the door "Inherit the century- old brand, Carry forward the traditional industry, March into the world market." After he was disinfected all over, Liang Shaozhong came to the nearest rough processing area where four workers were putting the flesh into the meat grinder. Within a few seconds, fish paste was squeezed out. Meanwhile, in the deep proceced area, workers were also performing their duties with great efficiency and accuracy. Compared to three decades ago, the efficiency is obviously greatly improved. A worker passed by with a trolley. Three boxes of just cooked fish balls, rounded and shiny, crunchy and tender, fresh and fragrant, bumped along with the locomotion of the trolley. Two different times and spaces seem to interplay due to similar fish balls. The distinctive recipe, craftsmanship and the lingering taste were passed on from Liang Zhibo to his son, Liang Shaozhong in this way.

Shantou, the special economic zone of Guangdong Province, is an important south-east coastal city. When it comes to Shantou, Chaoshan businessmen are widely known. Chaoshan businessmen group is one of the three traditional Chinese commercial groups, with its origin tracing back to the Ming Dynasty. Compared with the Shanxi Merchants and Huizhou Merchants, Chaoshan commercial group has prospered through long time and has the most influential impacts around the world. Where there is a tide, there are Chaoshan people. Where there is money to dig, there are Chaoshan businessmen. After five-hundred-years of commercial ups and downs, the Chaoshan business group has become the largest, most far-reaching and the only consecutive commercial group in China as well as the richest group among the Chinese community. They strongly believe that man with ambition is destined to great adventure in the business world. They are born with a talent for business. They are aggressive, bold and persistent. Numerous gold-digging scenes and commercial cases were created by Chaoshan

▲ Liang Shaozhong (right) participated in 2016 Singapore's Chaozhou Festival with his Jing Hua fish balls.

businessmen. Among the top 500 rich people on the "New Fortune" 2016 richest list, 36 of them are from Chaoshan, whose total assets reaching up to 689.59 billion yuan.

There are three rivers, Hanjiang, Rongjiang, and Lianjiang flowing into the sea in Shantou, with a mainland coastline of 217.7 km and an island coastline of 167.37 km. Dahao island is one of the 82 islands, which is rich in aquatic products and known for fish balls. Though it's not big, there are a dozen fish ball stores. "Jing Hua Fish Ball" excels in making finest fish balls, which helped them win the reputation of "Famous Chinese Cuisine". Inheriting the traditional ways of cooking, Jing Hua also creatively produces other products, such as shrimp balls, fish noodles, inkfish balls and so on. After tasting the Jing Hua fish balls, famous gourmet Wang Zengqi remarked: "If you haven't tasted the Jing Hua fish balls, you miss the chance to get to know Dahao."

Mr Liang Zhibo is the fourth chief master of the century-aged brand "Jing Hua Fish Ball" in Haojiang District, Shantou City. He inherited the essence of skills from previous ancestors and brought it into full play. Liang Shaozhong also took over his father's career just three years after his graduation from college. He explored how to make fish balls and how to manage the enterprise so that the family business could flourish from one generation to another.

"Jing Hua Fish Ball" was founded by Liang Jinghe more than 130 years ago. More than 100 years ago, it was just a snack bar, while the store's specialties were three balls - fish balls, shrimp balls and inkfish balls. In

2003, Chaoshan expatriat Chinese returned to their hometown and tasted the delicious fish balls. They brought the product back to the USA, which also captured the appetite of overseas Chinese. Soon, some people came to ask for cooperation with Liang Zhibo, hoping that those delicious fish balls could be exported to the USA. It occurred to Liang Zhibo to expand his business. To cater for the overseas market, Liang Zhibo established " Shantou Jinghua Minced Fish Food Factory Co., Ltd" . Currently, there are 13 chain stores in the mainland. Every morning, staffs of the stores go to the food factory to restock fresh fish balls. Meanwhile, in the United States, Hong Kong and other places, Jing Hua fish balls have also successfully appeared on supermarkets' shelves for sell.

Ambitious and Innovative Successor

Liang Shaozhong is the third child of Liang Zhibo's five children. Originally, the eldest son was set to take over the family enterprise and he majored in food processing in the university. But the eldest son gradually found that his interest lay in finance. Liang Zhibo did not had his son back but encouraged him to pursue what he loved as he himself always did before. As a result, Liang Shaozhong began to take on the heavy responsibility to facilitate the family career. Now, except that Liang Shaozhong is in charge of the family business, his brothers and sisters all work in banks or government institutions. Liang Shaozhong thinks his

▲ Liang Zhibo (middle) is teaching his son Liang Shaozhong (right) the skills of producing fish balls.

father has a profound influence on him and his sisters and brothers, that they can work on what they love and be successful in their fields respectively is contributed by the democratic growth environment and the best education resources provided by their father.

After graduating from university, Liang Shaozhong started to study the management of enterprise. With interest in business and passionate about traditional craftsmanship, he decided to take another road towards future though he majored in logistics in the university. He disagrees with the argument that only Japanese craftsmen are able to bring traditional craftsmanship into great achievements and thriving. He questioned why low-cost and poor quality products flooded the market. He wants to maintain and expand the brand "Jing Hua Fish Ball", to preserve this ancient craft, to enhance the value of fish balls and the value of the fish ball culture of the whole Dahao district, and to get more people impressed by Dahao fish balls. In December 2015, he went to Japan to study the advanced management experience and production craftsmanship. In March 2016, Liang Shaozhong and his "Jing Hua Fish Ball" brand were invited to attend the Chaozhou festival in Hong Kong by the Federation of Hong Kong Chiu Chow Chamber of Commerce. In October, the Hong Kong Government invited them to attend the food festival where Leung Chun-ying, the Chief Executive of the Hong Kong Special Administrative Region, tasted the fish balls in person and gave high comment. Leung Chun-ying's wife also bought a few bags of fish balls on the spot. At the same time, Liang Shaozhong expanded the business to e-commerce.

He opened shops on Taobao as well as other two large-scale electronic commercial platforms, which bring a profitable revenue every year. In order to make the fish balls purchased online remain fresh and sweet, he figured out an approach. First of all, he modified the packaging and storage methods. He imported new packaging materials which keep the storing temparature low long enough and inserts ice between the fish balls. In addition, he cooperates with the fastest delivery company, which ensures the customers can eat the freshest and finest fish balls on delivery. His move also benefits the fish ball stores in his hometown. Now, the new storage and packaging materials are widely used by fish ball stores in Dahao area.

Since Liang Shaozhong took over the business, he also encountered some barriers. The goal of "Jing Hua Fish Ball" is to make authentic Dahao fish balls, which requires the freshest fish. Over the years, they have insisted on using the fresh fish from nearby fishing ports. However, more than a decade ago, most areas of China began using frozen fish as raw ingredients, which not only reduces costs but also is conducive to storage and transportation. Even so, "Jing Hua Fish Ball" has not changed. They are strongly convinced that only fresh fish makes the finest and authentic Dahao fish balls.

The instability and scarcity of marine resources have a very large impact on fisheries. When the weather is bad or there are no fish, the fisherman have to rest and consequently, the production of fish balls also has to suspend. Because of the unstable supply of fish balls, Jing Hua Minced Fish Food Factory also missed a lot of golden opportunities. Both

Hong Kong PARKnSHOP and Guangdong Wong Chun Loong Traditional Chinese Herbal Tea had partnered with "Jing Hua Fish Ball". Unfortunately, the moody sea lessened the aquatic resources, which led to the termination of their cooperation.

But the biggest dilemma is the shortage of human resource. It takes a thousand times of pounding to make fish balls and fresh fish needs to be collected at a fixed time in early morning, which scares away many young people. On top of that, as the craftsmanship is passed on from ancestors, experience and skills are of crucial importance, which also makes the production of fish balls unfit for mass industrialized production according to general data and standards. That also resulted in the shortage of labour. But he believes that "Jing Hua Fish Ball" as a century-old brand through history and time, will stand still, despite great severe challenges. Jing Hua staffs will keep alert and get ready for embracing challenges.

Liang Shaozhong looks into the future with full expectations and plans. First of all, he would like to optimize the consumption mode of simply shopping online or at physical stores and turn it into a sustainable development model of consumption - tourism - and then consumption. He hopes to connect the local fish ball industry to tourism. He believes that through widespread publicity, more and more people will get to know Jing Hua fish balls. The purchase of Dahao Jing Hua fish balls may attract customers to visit Dahao personally where there are not only household fish balls, but also places of interests. Visitors may buy and bring fish balls back home after their visits or order aquatic products on the e-commerce platform. One move achieves multiple effects. "As Haojiang District is now developing towards a tourist city, without a doubt, the century-old brand 'Jing Hua Fish Ball' is sure to contribute its part. In the future, the headquarter may be restored to the model of 'having the store in front and the factory at back' as was done decades ago to attract customers by displaying its processing techniques", Liang Shaozhong said. As an entrepreneur of the last generation, Liang Zhibo has been adhering to the principle of "Good wine needs no bush", but in Liang Shaozhong's view, this principle does not work anymore in this era. So these days, "Jing Hua Fish Ball" has begun advertising itself and opened Weibo, while also adopts the prevailing method of "forward rewarding".

Liang Shaozhong also considered the matter of inheritance. That who the chief captain is does not matter, while what matters most is the craftsmanship of making Jing Hua fish balls and the family enterprise, especially its spirits need to be inherited and passed on.

He will not set demands and plans for his children in the future. He hopes his children can grow freely in a healthy environment and develop according to their own interests just as his father did for him. If the child loves this traditional craftsmanship and wants to carry it forward, he is happy to embrace the sixth generation of the successor of "Jing Hua Fish Ball". If the child is not interested in this industry, Liang Shaozhong will consider turning the company into a stock company and appointing a professional manager to carry on the business, in which way customers can always try and taste the authentic "Jing Hua Fish Ball".

Wu Hao and His
Haotian Bookstore

From Book Addictive Juvenile to Second-hand Book Seller

Located in Wende Sixth Alley, No. 148 Wenming Road, Yuexiu District, Guangzhou, the 50 square-meter Haotian Second-hand Bookstore is like a time collection museum preserving a frozen moment of the last century. Haotian bookstore seems detached from the massive changes of the outside world. The prevailing of digital reading like kindle or smartphone has squeezed the industry of paper book hard. Yet, Haotian bookstore stands still despite the massive changes of the outside world, like an old man hobbling alone. The running of a physical book store is more of a solemn and heroic action. Since it was opened in 1994 in Jiangxia Road, Baiyun District, the bookstore has been operated by Wu Hao for 23 years. Day after day, year after year, Wu Hao dedicated to treasuring his more than 30,000 second-hand books, sitting leisurely and quietly on the old cane chair.

In 1959, Wu Hao was born in a cottage in Wende Road, Yuexiu District of Guangzhou City where intellectual and litterateur prevailed since ancient times. As a street of culture and history, Wende Road is as famous as Beijing Liulichang, Shanghai Chenghuang Temple and Nanjing Confucius Temple. Along the road, there were antiques, ancient calligraphy and painting, ceramics and other stores, which dated back a long time. In Qing dynasty when the Imperial Examination System prevailed,

Guangzhou Gongyuan was built in Wende East Road with 5,000 dorms and served as county examination venue for Guangdong and Guangxi, which brought the business of antiques, paintings, selling of books and "four treasures of the study" into thriving. During the imperial examinations, thousands of examinees lingered in the market, appreciating or selecting treasures. What a prosperous scene! During the period of the Republic of China, there were 6 secondary schools, 10 bookstores and more than 10 cultural groups like Guangdong Western Returned Scholars Association here. After the People's Republic of China was founded, cultural groups with finest arts and assembly of talents-Provincial Dramatists Association, the Provincial Dancers Association, the Provincial Musicians Association, the Provincial Art Association all gathered here. Since the 1980s, Wende Road has been counted as one of the few very distinctive time-honored cultural specialized street of Lingnan Area.

▲ As Wu Hao was brought up in this street brimming with the fragrance of printing inks and books, surrounding by scholars, he became having an affinity towards books since childhood.

As Wu Hao was brought up in this street brimming with the fragrance of printing inks and books, surrounding by scholars, he became having an affinity towards books since childhood. Back to days at No.3 primary school in Wende North road, the Guangzhou Children's Library next to the school was just his paradise. Everytime he went off school, the little boy would get into the reading room, hold one and another comic book and devour them. Once, Wu Hao was fascinated by one comic book and he couldn't tear himself away from it. At that time, a book cost fifteen cents and a breakfast cost six cents. In order to put his hand on it, He starved himself for consecutive three mornings and finally saved enough money and got the comic book from the children' bookstore near the Youth Culture Palace. He brought it back home and began copying it. His addiction to books is by no means less than today's juvenile's addiction to the internet. After the initial sweetness, the book addictive juvenile began pondering how to make money in return for books. Eventually, he came up with the idea of picking up orange peels. In traditional Chinese medicine, dried orange peel is called dried tangerine peel. Guangdong people are used to cooking soup with dried tangerine peel or putting it into medicine, which is said to be able to replenish *qi* and invigorate the spleen function and dissolve phlegm. Every weekend, Wu Hao would go collecting orange peels from the trash cans in the streets and exchange happily a small bag of orange peels for money at the garbage collection station. A month's hard work would be enough to exchange for a comic book. At that time, to eat their fill and dress warmly were the fundamental demand of the Chinese people when everything was in great shortage. Besides, Wu Hao's parents are illiterate. To ask them to buy a book for the kid is like wanting a pie in the sky. Wu Hao saved every penny to buy books, from which his business mind also flourished. It's just the books he reached at that time seemed far from enough for this big fish to swim in. In that age, books contributed four great inventions to "working people", but without a word on who those "working people" were. Thirty or forty years before the advent of Google, Baidu, that knowledge can only be sought from the old history books. Bidding farewell to childhood addiction to comics, young man Wu Hao turned to old books.

On August 9, 1955, Beijing youth Yang Hua, Li Bingheng and other people proposed to the Communist Youth League Beijing Committee to reclaim wasteland in the border areas. Their proposal was immediately approved and encouraged in November. That scholars, college students and intellectuals went to the countryside to reclaim wasteland was catching on in China subsequently. Chairman Mao instructed "Rural area is a vast world, where one's ability can be developed to the full", "It's of great necessity for intellectuals and college students to be spread to the countryside and be educated by poor and lower-middle class peasants". The Chinese government called on a multitude of urban "intellectual youth" to leave the city and launched the Mass-Line-Movement of settling and labouring in rural areas. In 1977, Wu Hao graduated from senior high school and was assigned to Aotou Town, Conghua City (now Conghua District of Guzngzhou). In October 1978, the Chinese government decided to halt the movement of "Educated Youth Went to and Worked in Countryside and Mountain Areas" and resettle their return and employment properly. After 1979, the majority of educated youths returned to cities. So did Wu Hao. He returned to Guangzhou, but his household registration was registered in the countryside. Without a household registration in Guangzhou, he couldn't be assigned a job. In order to make a living, Wu Hao came up with the idea of printing books and selling them by himself. He first bought a reference book on how to make copies on the mimeograph in a second-hand bookstore on Beijing Road. The so-called mimeo is to first cover a wax paper on the steel plate and then carve above it with an iron pen. After inking the wax paper above a printing paper, copies can be printed. Wu Hao loved listening to Hongkong radio at that time, which was not permitted under the then political environment. He could only turn on the radio after 12 o'clock in the midnight. Lying on the table, he recorded what he heard while listening until two or three o'clock in the morning. He carved the characters, printed the content into two hundred pieces and bound them. Thus books on maxims of celebrities and styles of conversation were brought to sell at the gate of the Xinhua Bookstore on Beijing road. These rare books soon became best-sellers. He sold these books at 50 cents each, whose printing cost was only 5 cents each. Within a few days, Wu Hao made a bundle selling out all the books. But when he was ready to close the stall, two staffs from the government stopped him and brought him to the police station due to his action of "speculation". Fortunately, the police just criticised him and made him reflect on his action overnight, then released him without confiscating his earnings. Wu Hao returned home joyfully. After the initial savour of sweetness, he began to understand people's thirst for books and knowledge. He did not dare to print books by himself. Thus he started doing business in another way——selling books. Soon after he was educated at the police station, Xinhua Bookstore began selling stored books, for instance, Tang poetry, world-famous masterpieces, which were prohibited over the past decade. Intellectuals at that time were no less crazy about books than today's young people for their idols. The spectacular scene of nabbing books took place every day in Xinhua Bookstore. As demand outstrips supply, Xinhua Bookstore regulated that each person was allowed to buy only two sets of books per day and those books were selected at random. Wu Hao perceived the potential business opportunity. Being at an idle end, he waited from two or three o'clock in the morning in front of Xinhua Bookstore. Every day at 9 am when Xinhua Bookstore opened, it was a way long queue. But Wu Hao always stood in the head of the line and he could get his hand on two sets of books, namely 4 to 8 books. Wu Hao would then sell the books on the market at thirteen or fourteen yuan a set, which cost him 5 to 6 yuan initially. He earned over 100 yuan after a dozen of days. After the stored books of Xinhua Bookstore were sold out, Wu Hao had to figure out another way to make money. From then on, he became a "broker" in Tian Guang Xu, in his words, a special profession beyond the well-known seventy-two occupations in China. Tian Guang Xu stands for the folk flea market in Guangzhou. As it starts operating ere morning or at midnight and ends at the dawn, so it is named "Tian Guang Xu" (In Cantonese, Tian Guang means dawn), a noun appearing only in Cantonese. "Tian Guang Xu" reached its heyday at the end of Qing Dynasty and the beginning of Republic of China where mainly old furniture, utensils, clothing, and other second-hand cheap goods and antiques, calligraphy and painting, ancient books, potteries, etc were traded. Nowadays, the state of operation of such markets differs from one to another. "Tian Guang Xu" in Haizhu Zhong Road where secondhand books are traded still opens every Saturday. "Flee Market" in Binjiang Road runs from morning to noon every day. "Flower Market" in Fangcun West Avenue opens only in the wee hours of the morning. "Tian Guang Xu" in Wenchang Road where cultural relics are traded opens on every Tuesday morning. "Tian Guang Xu" in Hualin where jades are traded are currently renovating. And the second-hand market in Liwan Road where old electronic products were traded had already gone. 20-year- old Wu Hao wandered in "Tian Guang Xu" in Haizhu Zhong Road and Wenchang Road and made a handsome profit by reselling second-hand books, which is anything but less than his friends' stable incomes.

Exploring "Ten-Year Plan"

In 1980, Wu Hao's household registration moved back to Guangzhou. In the views of most people, it's rational to have a stable job, which also stands for social status. Thus, Wu Hao became a first-class worker at the Eighth Machinery factory of Guangzhou, earning a monthly salary of more than 30 yuan. At that time, China has carried out reform and opening-up. On December 11, 1980, 19-year-old Zhang Huamei from Wenzhou City, Zhejiang Province received a special business license from the Wenzhou Administration for Industry and Commerce. This license, written in ink brush and enclosed with a photo, is the first individual business license in China and Zhang Huamei has become China's first individual industrial and commercial household. And in Guangzhou, Rong Zhiren, who was born in a family of intellectuals, opened a "Rong Guang" restaurant near his home. In the early 1980s, his restaurant earned one or two hundred yuan per day. Sometimes, the restaurant could sell up to 300 pounds of "Changfen" a day. In 1981, as one of the representatives of individual commercial households, Rong Zhiren was received and hosted by the provincial party secretary Ren Zhongyi and then elected as president of Guangzhou Individual Worker's Association. After that, he was hosted by Deng Xiaoping and Hu Yaobang consequently, which became a startup story on everyone's lip. And in Gaodi Street, Guangzhou, quite a number of households who made more than 10 thousand yuan have sprung up. Wu

Hao, who was always sharp in mind and insights, began to wear out patience. In 1987, he gave up the "iron rice bowl" - secure employment and threw himself into the mainstream of the market economy. This was his only experience deviated from second-hand books and antiques during his business career. At that time, the business of frames of mirrors or glasses were flourishing in Wende Road. To engage in those business costs a great deal of investment. Besides, it's not easy to get a slice of the rationed cake. Wu Hao thought: "Since I cannot compete with you, I can cooperate with you." Then he engaged himself in transport. The glasses frames and mirror frames in Wende Road were mainly sold to Hongkong. Wu Hao raked together 10,000 yuan, bought a truck of output volume of 0.6 litres and began doing business with frame store owners. Every time frame stores received new orders, he would go to the factory to load goods and send them directly to the port. The daily revenue could reach 100 yuan. Deducting the costs, he could earn over 50 yuan. The monthly net profit of fifteen or sixteen hundred yuan was absolutely high income at that time. After doing the transport for seven years, Wu Hao accumulated enough capital and once again he turned to his old livelihood - selling books. Born and brought up in Wende Road, Wu Hao, who neighbored a library, has a lingering connection with books. Wende Road use to be a street where mainly books were traded. During the most prosperous time, there were more than 30 bookstores on the street. Since childhood, Wu Hao had dreamed of opening his own bookstore. Wu Hao took the strategy of "Encircling the rural areas from the cities". In the 1980s, Xi Juan, Qiong

Yao's romance novels and martial arts novels of Gu Long, Jin Yong have been popular in the mainland. At that time, the entertainment was still very scarce. In addition to watching TV, people loved reading novels most during their spare time. One's life couldn't be happier than holding a novel in his or her hands and appreciating the happiness and sadness of young heroes and heroines or the boldness of swordsman. In the suburb linking the urban and rural area in Guangzhou, there were only a few bookstores. It took a lot of trouble for young people to go to the cities and buy books. Besides, the novels can be read through within two or three days. Most of the young man could not afford to buy books one after one.In 1994, Wu Hao moved to Huangshi Road in Baiyun District from Wende Road. He had his first "Hao Tian Bookstore" in front and his home behind, which specifically sells and rents all kinds of books. It cost fifty cents to rent one book for a day. For a moment, Hao Tian Bookstore was full of customers and prosperous in business, with its daily revenue reaching up to 300 yuan.

Hao Tian Bookstore had been in Huangshi Road for seven years. Wu Hao did not move back to Wenming Road until 2003, which is one block away from his old house. By that time, the book market has plunged sharply. Within a few years, a number of popular bookstores came to close successively in Guangzhou. Despite widespread lamentation, Chinese people did read less and less. Hao Tian Bookstore was no exception and business was dull. However, Wu Hao is full of confidence with his "Second Ten-Year Plan". "Long before I had this triple ten-year plan. The first ten-year plan has been achieved, that is, selling books and renting out books.

The second ten-year plan is to do niche market. Now everybody is competing for price reductions. I do not follow the crowd. What I do is the niche market. The third ten-year plan is to do a miniature museum. I am not as restless as others. I am cool as I have my own plan." The niche market Wu Hao pursues, in fact, is his old career, namely, scrapping up rare collections in Tian Guang Xu. These few years, Hao Tian Bookstore became one of the distinctive second-hand bookstores on the tongue of Guangzhou. And he has done several superb deals. He had once discovered a couplet by Qing Dynasty poet Zhang Weiping in Tian Guang Xu. He bought the couplet at 300 yuan and finally sold it out at 3000 yuan, which is ten times of the price. He also acclaimed that he collected a Buddhist scripture dating back to the reign of Emperor Kangxi, which he deemed "the representative piece of his collections". He bought it at 500 yuan. Wu Hao is confident on his discernment in telling the counterfeits from the authentic works. He explained the reason why the Buddhist scripture is originated from Qing Dynasty is that the paper of Qing Dynasty was more transparent and had a close texture while modern paper production has no longer produced such kind of paper. This Buddhist scripture is now preserved at Wu's house. "This is a treasure, waiting for the highest bid. I am not in a hurry to sell it. Rarely do I mention it with others."

Dealing with second-hand books for years, Wu Hao has been adroit at repairing old books. He re-nailed the cover for books or put them behind a transparent protective cover. Some paper sheets have been dried and brittle over years. He used protective layers to cover them one sheet after another.

To boost selling, Wu Hao and his wife bought a computer and opened an online shop on Confucius Second-hand Book Net-China's largest second-hand book online trading market. However, lacking web maintenance techniques has become a big trouble for them. Every time they come across a website crash, the couple felt helpless and overwhelmed. The online shop needs design, updating

▲ Wu Hao's third ten-year plan is to turn "Haotian" to a miniature museum. Today, "Haotian" is highly exalted by literary and artistic youth in the city.

the contents regularly and web maintenance, which requires thousands of yuan to hire technicians. The couple was overwhelmed by numerous trifles of the operation of the online shop, which even affects the healthy operation of the physical bookstore. Six months later, "Haotian" online bookstore ended up closing.

Wu Hao's third ten-year plan is to turn "Haotian" to a miniature museum. Today, "Haotian" is highly exalted by literary and artistic youth in the city. Wu Hao designed the layout and details all by himself. Except all kinds of second-hand books, the inactive clock hanging in the center of bookstore, the old-fashioned basket dangling from the ceiling, the old accordion, the scales and the previous film stubs, collection of coins in the shopping window, the enamel basin prevailing in the 1950s, 1960s as well as the green military kettle placed on the bookcase, were delicately arranged and were collected from Tian Guang Xu by Wu Hao every week. Several young people are wandering in the store. They are more coming here to take pictures than buying books. Nowadays, posting pictures in the Moments of Wechat is what the youth love to do, by which they express their universal affection for literary or arts. Seeing that, Wu Hao can only shrug and smile. Reality belittles his ambition. Nowadays, Haotian

▲ Regular patron was reading at Haotian Bookstore.

Bookstore merely struggles to make ends meet. The distinctive Haotian Bookstore attracts many a young people to visit. Yet, most of them come here just to take several pictures or buy a few postcards. Few of them would buy books. Observing the situation, Mrs Luo, Wu Hao's wife, is coming to worry about its future and sometimes she gets irritated. At her insistence, "Haotian" established a "rule" that photographing is prohibited without shopping. In Mrs.Luo's words, "Doing business is not easy. At least the unique experience is worth paying." Wu Hao is too shy to ban visitors taking pictures, let alone, asking them to buy products. When his wife is not in the store, he would sit on the cane chair quietly, allowing the young people to take pictures freely. Every time his wife happens to come back and see it, she could not help becoming angry. There are also some ill remarks on the internet like the interview fee with Haotian is 100 yuan per hour. This is the rule set by Mrs Luo. But you can also choose to buy some products from the bookstore in exchange for an interview. The sum is not required and at interviewer's disposal. If you do not buy anything, the interview fee is 100 yuan per hour.

Wu Hao respects Mrs Luo and everything is at her call. He could only smile and apologise: "I am sorry. Thank you for your understanding." "If he accepts your interview, he would have no time to take care of the business. Many times, our books got stolen. Some young people came and left with our postcards. When I stopped them, they excused that they didn't know that they have to pay. We are struggling to make a living. We have no means to survive if we do not behave like this." A sense of grievance underlay between her words. Wu Hao remains silent by the side. The young man Wu Hao held great ambition to make a living and a career on books. Today, he is more carrying on the spirit of an old man sticking to operate a bookstore. He has dedicated himself to books for over two decades. Now he is coming to hesitate to retreat before his ambition gets achieved and prepare to leave the bookstore at his wife's care. Some people used "Utopia in the cultural desert" to describe "Haotian". In face of the surging wave of the Internet, the entrepreneur Wu is more like Don Quixote fighting against the windmill. Can bread and dream coexist? May Guangzhou "Haotian" stand still in the next decade.

Zhou Chong:
I am " Propping up
Bro".

Make a Living as a Blue Collar

On June 3, 2012, in order to rescue a little girl dangling on the anti-theft bar of the balcony, Zhou Chong clambered out of a building's third floor's anti-theft window escape exit and propped the girl up with one hand, whose action saved essential time for rescue work. The six-minute action changed the life of Zhou Chong. He rose to fame from a worried man hunting for a job and won numerous acclaim. Not only did he get a job, but also he got the household registration of Guangzhou. If you input "Zhou Chong" in Baidu News, the first pop-up is that on March 24, 2016, "Technician Zhou Chong was elected vice chairman of Guangdong Youth Federation." Except for admiration, many people would envy that Zhou Chong is fortunate. But in fact, he could have been better off. When great opportunities like manager, director with over ten thousands yuan monthly salary knocked on his door, he chose to be himself and became a maintenance worker at Guangzhou Port Group. This does not mean that he has no ambition. What he wants is just to do what he is capable of and rely on his own ability to achieve the advancement of career and life. "I do not want to be commented behind. Neither do my parents. They called me every day to tell me to be down-to-earth. I heard so much that cocoons already showed up in my ears." Five years passed, Zhou Chong has never regretted his choice. Speaking of that sensational action of propping up the little girl five years ago, he still humbly deems it a small deed. But when it comes to working, his words fail to conceal his self-confidence. "I have been in this post for five years, no one ever doubted my ability." Five years ago, Zhou Chong propped one life up with his hands. Zhou Chong builds his own life and future with the same hands in the past, now and in the future.

In 1989, at Zhouxiang town, Xiaochang County, Xiaogan city, Hubei Province, Zhou Yuming and Song Xiuying embraced their first child. The boy looked strong and cute as a tiger, with single eyelids and his eyes are small around, full of energy and spirit. Zhou Yuming couple looked at this clever-looked child, full of joy, and named him "Zhou Chong", with the hope that he has the momentum to lead a bright future. However, life didn't go as smoothly as they expected. They led a poor life. Zhong Chong's father had to go to the city for a long time to take part-time jobs and tried to make a living. When Zhong Chong was a child, he rarely saw his father and could only depend on his mom. Later on, his younger brother and sister were born successively. It was even harder to make ends meet. When it's time for the three kids to go to school and pay for tuition fee, Zhou Chong's father would be frantic with worry and couldn't help smoking to inhibit his worry. As the eldest child among three, Zhou Chong began to take some responsibility and help relieve his parents' work at the age of 13. He is good at all kinds of farming work like transplanting rice seedlings, reaping rice and pulling the wood cart. In 2005, he graduated from junior high school. Without the hope to enter a key high school, he went to Guangzhou and turned to his cousin. Through someone's introduction, he became a shopping guide in a supermarket in Yuancun. 19 days later, he got his first salary of 200 yuan. When he first came to Guangzhou, Zhou Chong only spent 2 yuan on eating stir-fried rice noodles every weekend. Otherwise, he won't spare any penny. His boss provided lodging and meals for him. Zhou Chong saved 200 yuan and planned to bring the 200 yuan to his parents during the spring festival. At that time, he had no concept of money. For him, 200 yuan leads to hope. He was thinking since he can save 200 yuan within 19 days, he can save up to 4000 after a year. With this amount of money, his parents don't have to be so hard on themselves anymore. However, after working for more than three months, for the first time, he hung out with his roommate in Guangzhou's shopping malls, only to find the world is not like what he imagined. He found it cost him one month's salary to buy even one of the most common shirts in the TEEMALL. Since then, he rarely went out and buried himself into work. However, no matter how hard he worked, he still felt he was at the edge of the city in his deep heart as he earns little and owns no techniques. There was no chance to seize those high-salary positions and he couldn't see any hope of development. Zhou Chong did not want to waste time in struggling at the bottom of the society. So he decided to leave Guangzhou and went to learn welding from his uncle in Guizhou. At the end of 2005, after half a year's working in Guangzhou, Zhou Chong settled up the wages with his boss and went back home sadly. A 16-year-old boy's dream about the big city ended before it got started.

A few days after he got back home, Zhou Chong could scarcely keep in. His horizon has been opened while his current situation made him anxious. Eager to change, he brought around 300 yuan of transportation fee and went to Guizhou before the celebration of Spring Festival. His Uncle introduced him to a welder in Zunyi. He worked as an apprentice without salary, except lodging and meals were provided. Although conditions were harsh, Zhou agreed. In the following year, Zhou Chong got up at 4 o'clock in the morning every day and started working at 4:30am. He had to lift iron box and cut metal before 8am to catch up breakfast in the morning. Then, He worked until 2pm for lunch, and he had to work overtime until the wee hours of the morning. From 2006 to 2007, it was the most difficult time in Zhong Chong's life. He was so exhausted that he could even fall asleep sitting. He did not have the strength to think too much under such intensive work. As his master was mosthy taking personal maintenance job, he did not learn much about practical welding techniques. But two senior fellow disciples let Zhou Chong operate the welding machine from time to time, in which way he had the chance to operate it for a few times. Life is so hard that he could not even afford one bottle of shampoo. Once he couldn't stand his itchy scalp anymore and he grabbed a clump of washing powder, applied it to the head and washed the hair. In such an extremely difficult circumstance, Zhou Chong stuck to it for two years. In early 2008, holding 500 yuan of wages, he once again embarked on the road home. What is different from two years ago is that now he has commanded techniques. He felt more determined and certain than two years ago. Soon, he got a job as a welder in a construction site in Hanjiang district, Wuhan city. Within four years, his salary rose from 1,000 yuan to more than 5,000 yuan. With the "core competitiveness" within him, he began to plan his future and decided to be a contractor. He contracts projects and calls on his countrymen to work for it. In his plan, he can even be a boss in the future. That year, he was 23 years old. The world unfolded in front of him and he saw unlimited opportunities and endless possibilities. He thought he would create his own career in Wuhan. Yet, he did not predict he would be attached to this city, Guangzhou, again.

In March 2012, Zhou Chong's father Zhou Yuming helped with house decoration for a family in the neighboring village. Zhou Chong also went back to help temporarily due to lack of manpower. That family's daughter Li Ying, who worked in Guangzhou, also came back home and help with interior decoration. For the first meeting, Zhou Chong fell in love with the girl with big eyes. Li Ying also developed an affinity towards Zhong Chong, an energetic young man. However, the distance between Wuhan and Guangzhou made Li Ying feel quite hesitant. In order to dispel the girl's concern, Zhou Chong decided to quit his job and follow her to return to Guangzhou. Zhong Chong's boss really appreciated this honest and diligent young man. Knowing that Zhou Chong would rather give up this salary-competitive job for a girl, he then advised him, "Now it is not easy to find a job of 5000 yuan a month. Who knows what the situation will be when you arrives in Guangzhou. If you can not find a job, is the girl willing to be with you?" Zhou Chong was determined:"If I am into something, for sure I will stick to it. " His sincerity and courage impressed Li Ying. Soon they confirmed the relationship of boyfriend and girlfriend. On May 22, 2012, Zhou Chong with his girlfriend, returned back to Guangzhou, the city he left seven years ago. However, although he commanded techniques, the process of looking for a job was not as smooth as he'd expected. As he came to Guangzhou, he had to start everything from scratch. Others did not know about his ability either. Some would tell him that he was too young without any experience. Others replied they had recruited the people they wanted. In desperation, Zhou Chong had no choice but help his cousin temporarily to take care of his store. He attended to the shop from noon to midnight every day. He started looking for a job outside at 7 or 8 o' clock in the morning.

Propping up Bro

On June 3, 2012, Zhou Chong was accompanying his girlfriend to look for a job in Dongpu when a little girl named Qiqi got trapped in the balcony railings of a fourth-floor apartment. It's at this heart-stopping moment that Zhou Chong risked his life and clambered out of the third-storey window to prop up Qiqi for up to 8 minutes, which led to an about-face in his life. Nanfang Metropolis Daily reporter Xie Zhenhui recorded this shocking and heart-stopping scene. Qiqi, then three, was left home alone after the door was locked, and was trying to get out. She climbed the mainframe of the air conditioner in the balcony of the room and then climbed the parapet of the balcony whose height is even higher than that of her, trying to climb into the study room next door. However, she slipped through an aluminum flower rack which is just narrow enough to catch her head, with her body dangling in the air.

At 11:30, a passer-by heard cries above the head and looked up to find a child dangling from the balcony and exclaimed, "There is a kid about to fall down." Hearing it, neighbors all came swiftly. Several men rushed to the place below Qiqi and stretched out hands in the gesture of propping up, for fear that the child would fall down. There are neighbors running upstairs quickly, knocking heavily on the door of Qiqi's apartment, but no one answered.

At 11:31, one shop owner downstairs got three cartons and placed them on the ground in case the little girl falls, hoping them to play the role as a buffer and avoid greater harm. A couple on the spot went home to fetch a yellow bed sheet and rushed all the way back to the scene. 4 men immediately unfolded it in four corners underneath, ready to catch Qiqi. Learning the news, a kind-hearted woman, Mrs.Pan, rapidly unlocked the anti-theft window so that the neighborhood could get out to rescue the little girl. Zhou Chong who was passing by also followed those kind-hearted neighborhoods into Mrs.Pan's home.

At 11:32, Mr. Zhou, a cleaner at Yidongyuan residential community moved two mattresses out of their home and placed them on the ground right below the bed sheet, with his wife.

At 11:35, Huang Hanchu, a traffic policeman of the Tianhe area, came to the spot. He requested for support with a walkie-talkie immediately while examining the situation. On the other hand, several men tried to climb out of the anti-theft window downside of Qiqi to save her but failed due to the narrow gaps between the anti-theft window bars at Pan's. At this time, Qiqi was almost strengthless so that her hands initially holding the flower rack loosened, her head still stuck in the railings, as if she was hung.

CC-TV shows that at 11:36, Zhong Chong in yellow shirt climbed the anti-theft window of the 3rd floor. At that time, the flower rack just stuck Qiqi's throat. The child's tears have been run out, her mouth beginning to show white foam. While Zhou Chong stood on his toes on the bottom of the anti-theft window, he is not tall enough to prop up

Qiqi's feet with strength. He scaled a grip up to enable Qiqi to step on his hand and get her head out of the flower rack. Subsequently, Qiqi recovered her strength and began to cry again. Zhou Chong then climbed to the third grid of the anti-theft window bar. He propped her up with his right hand while standing on his toes and clinging to the outside wall of the building with his left hand. A neighbor fetched a rope and tied it to Zhou Chong's waist and another man held Zhou Chong's feet through the window in case he fell.

At 11:42, Qiu Renxian, deputy squadron chief at Dongpu squadron of Tianhee traffic police brigade, arrived at the spot from an accident scene in Chepei. At his command, the neighbors broke in Qiqi's house to rescue Qiqi's life.

At 11:45, the flower rack was sawed off. The frightened Qiqi sank into her grandpa's arms, surrounded by a round of applause. Meanwhile, Zhou Chong quietly climbed down the anti-theft window and left the scene with Li Ying and his nephew without commenting on the incident.

However, Zhou Chong's figure has been captured by the surveillance camera and videos taken by the public spontaneously. His rescue move went viral on the internet. Guangzhou launched a search throughout the city. Various social media posted missing person notice through televisions: " Height of about 1 meter 78 cm, burly, non-native of Guangzhou. Anyone who has information about this man can contact the neighborhood committee of Tianhe district. Relevant rewards are expected to be presented to this man." The China Twitter Sina Weibo also posted a "good man wanted": Time: 11:30 am on June 3rd; Spot: Yidongyuan residential community in Dongpu, Tianhe district; Matter: 3-year-old girl, Qiqi was dangling from the fourth floor balcony by neck and a man in yellow shirt risked his life to prop up the child until she was rescued. He left without any news. Do you know where he is? Everyone, please help find him. At the same time, there were people who were against the search, "Since he wants only his action to be ascribed in people's heart, why is it necessary to dig out his identity?""It doesn't matter who he is. What counts is the spirit. The internet mass hunting would only distort the initial intention of the rescuer and make people suspect his motive, thinking that he wants to get the spotlight."

On June 9, Zhou Chong was found by the media. One interview after another, his face was recognized and remembered by countless people. People affectionately called him "Prop up bro". His deeds were also reported on the CCTV News. He became a household civil hero in Guangzhou in 2012. Zhou Chong was overwhelmed by all this. He did not know "Xiao Yue Yue incident" that occurred a half year ago in Foshan, an indelible pain for Guangdong citizens as he had been in Guangzhou for less than 20 days. On October 13 2011, 2-year-old little girl Yueyue was run over by two cars successively, in which scene 18 pedestrian passengers ignored the injured child and walked away within 7 minutes, before Chen Xianmei, a 57 years old female ragpicker, noticed the child while she was collecting trash, came forward to help and pick Yueyue up in Nanhai Huangqi Guangfo Hardware City, Foshan. The chilling view recorded by surveillance cameras shocked viewers in the world and turned the guts of Chinese upside-down. On October 21, 2011, "Xiao Yue Yue" was announced to be dead at 00:32 am by the hospital after doctors tried to keep her alive but was to no avail. On October 23, 2011, 280 citizens of Foshan gathered at the incident site to pay tribute to "Xiao Yue Yue", through candle lighting and opposed being "cold apathy Foshaner". On October 29, 2011, with memorial service and farewell ceremony, Xiao Yueyue's body was cremated in Guangzhou funeral parlour and her ashes were brought back home to Shandong.

The society was in urgent need of positive energy and Zhou Chong's appearance as well as the neighbors, like a light in the darkness, illuminated the hearts of people.

On June 13, 2012, the then Member of the CPC Central Committee Political Bureau, member of the Secretariat of the CPC Central Committee, Minister of the Publicity Department of the Communist Party of China, Deputy Director of the Central Civilization Committee, Liu Yunshan, received and hosted representatives of models from all over the country, Zhou Chong was on the list.

A Welder

Compared with honors and rewards, what surprised Zhou Chong most was the ensuing job opportunities. Just within two days, he received employment invitations from 11 state- owned enterprises in Guangzhou, while some of them he would never expect before. "There is a very well-known real estate company who invited me to be a deputy manager, responsible for the operation and supervision of field projects. There is also an institution willing to recruit me as vice director of the general office, responsible for the management of the entire park' s sanitation and security work, which offers over ten thousand yuan monthly salary, a separate office, and a dormitory with one bedroom, one living room, as well as private car pick up service." For Zhou Chong, those unexpected and admirable job opportunities were no mere tempting. However, he eventually chose to become a welder in Guangzhou Port Group. In contrast, this job is more arduous and demands high techniques and even may cause some detriment to the body. The remuneration is by no means inviting. But what matters is that he can live with a good conscience and enjoy it. Rising to fame, the media also flocked to his hometown for interviewing with his parents. Zhou Chong's parents were happy but also worried. During that period of time, Zhou Yuming called his son every day and asked him to accept a job matching his own ability lest others would gossip. Being persons of integrity, the Zhou Yuming couple were afraid of being gossiped most. The

▲ The welding work was tailored for Zhou Chong. He had been doing welding work for six years. Moreover, the Guangzhou Port Group has developed a series of training programs for him, in which position, he can develop his own ability.

same words repeated over and over again. Zhou Chong's ears heard them so many times that he joked cocoon has grown in his ears. But eventually, he took his parent's advice. Apart from remuneration, he thought more about whether he is competent and capable in that position. Yet the welding work was tailored for Zhou Chong. He had been doing welding work for six years. Moreover, the Guangzhou Port Group has developed a series of training programs for him, in which position, he can develop his own ability. If he rushed to accept a job as manager, he certainly could not convince the public. How can he occupy the position belonging to someone else who made over ten years' efforts for this position while he merely propped up a little girl for dozens of minutes?

Being a welder, Zhou Chong is tough and confident. He is honest and down-to-earth in every step. He made use of his spare time to attend classes at Guangzhou Port Technical School. In June 2015, he successfully got his technical secondary school diploma. Then he signed up for a junior college's courses on mechanical integration. In the future, he will try to get an undergraduate diploma. His life plan is very clear. He will learn some management knowledge during the undergraduate program and try his best to get a master's degree before 35 years old. In 2014, Zhou Chong won the first prize in the competition of second-class welding maintenance held by the Guangzhou Port Group, he then got promoted as a senior welder. In 2015, he was rated as a model worker at Guangdong provincial level due to his prominent work performance. "I have been working at this position for five years. No one had ever criticized my work. I can cope with most of the maintenance on my own." Zhou Chong's resdential place is a company's dormitory which is 3 kilometers or so from the port. As the event cooled down, he began to lead a peaceful and fulfilling life. At 7:15am, He rides a bike to the company. At 7:30am or so, he gets to the company. Around 7:45-7:50am, they have a meeting before work where the head of the squadron arranges the day's work. Then everyone goes to work. If there is no welding maintenance work, Zhou Chong would do some basic maintenance or assist the head of the squadron to categorize files and some other basic management works. At 11:45am, it is time for him to have lunch. If there is urgent maintenance work left, he would grab a bite before starting work. Generally, he starts working at 14:00 in the afternoon until 17:00 and then gets off. Over the past few years since his name became a household name, Zhou Chong went to a lot of universities to do lectures in which the question asked most frequently by young people is whether he had changed his girlfriend, which made him pull a wry face every time. Zhong Chong and Li Ying got married in April 2013 and now they have a two-year-old daughter. His wife is a documentation clerk. The double-income add up to no more than ten thousand yuan a month, which is not low but far from enough to afford an apartment in Guangzhou. Zhou Chong is recently saving money to buy an apartment. For many migrant workers, one can not call himself Cantons without buying a residential place in Guangzhou even if he manages to get Guangzhou household registration. Zhou Chong never hides his "ambition" and he is never satisfied to restrict himself to be a welder during his life. Now he keeps learning and hopes that he can take up the management position one day. "We must dream and dream big. How can a person be aimless without a dream?"

Man Committed to
Public Welfare

In March 2016, Zhong Chong's name once again appeared in the newspaper, after gradually faded from the public's attention. On March 23, *Guangzhou Daily* reported that on the Fourth Session of the Standing Committee (enlarged) of the Tenth Guangdong Provincial Youth Federation which was held in Guangzhou, young technician Zhong Chong, "the propping up bro" and Guangdong Provincial Youth "Wusi" medalist, was elected as the provincial vice chairman of the Youth Federation. Guangdong Provincial Youth Federation and public welfare are closely related. Since he became the "propping up bro" in 2012, Zhou Chong began to become attached to the public welfare activities. Initially, he had no concept of "public welfare". At that time, he just rose to fame and many institutions both from Guangdong and other provinces invited him to attend activities, which requires permission of the company. Once approved by his leader at the group, he had to go. He was absent half a month during one month's shift for attending activities. At the beginning, he felt exhausted and a sense of guilt to his colleagues. He didn't get touched by soul until Sep. 2013 when he attended one activity to help the poor. He began to understand what his action means to those people in need not until then. It was at one poverty alleviation activity in a village in Qingyuan. Dozens of people got off the car and came to a brick house,

which has no gate. Inside there are a few huts even without a decent door, but a curtain braced by two pieces of wood. Heard the sound, a skinny and humpback old man stumbled from the hut. Volunteers moved the rice, oil, and quilt into the hut. The old man held Zhou Chong's hand, his tears clapping down, which fell right on Zhou Chong's hands. At that time, Zhou Chong cried bitterly. From then on, every time he mentions his road to public welfare, he would bring up this experience. Since 2012, Zhou Chong began to participate in various volunteer services and

▲ Since 2012, Zhou Chong began to participate in various volunteer services and charity activities. Until today, he takes part in no less than 200 public welfare activities in his spare time.

charity activities. Until today, he takes part in no less than 200 public welfare activities in his spare time. A volunteer center in Huangpu District was named after him. In Tianhe district, there are also volunteer centers which go after Zhou Chong's name. In addition to work, study and rest, Zhou Chong almost spent the rest of his time on public welfare. He also stimulates his family to do public service. His wife, for instance, often joins him in distributing public welfare leaflets in her spare time. A hero's aura can drive the community and call on everyone to help others. But each of us as a part of the society, no matter with fame or not, should contribute to the society from every aspect. Zhou Chong expressed that regardless of him being famous or not in the future, he still hopes to influence and motivates people around and make everyone see the positive energy of the society through his hands.

Flow upward

Migrant Workers Got Admission into Peking University

On September 29, 2012, Guangzhou Migrant Worker Museum was opened. Guangzhou Migrant Worker Museum, the first official museum of its kind in China, is located in Mawu village, Guangzhou' s Baiyun district and tells the stories of migrant workers through about 5,000 pieces of physical objects. The museum is housed in No. 12 of a renovated former village- run industrial park named Lianhe launched in the 1980s in Mawu of Baiyun district to house export-oriented factories, centred on which, the Guangzhou City Impression Park was built. It displays the development and change of migrant worker's lives and working conditions over the past

▲ Migrant workers have made an indelible contribution to the construction of Guangdong.

three decades. The four-storeies pavilion is themed "general preface""birth and development""approaching hundreds of millions of migrant workers" respectively, reflecting the history, work and life of migrant workers comprehensively. The reproduction of original workshop in the first floor "moves" the completed shoe and garment production lines into the museum. Below the banner "Security is of most importance, heavier than Mount Tai", a large number of sewing machines, machinery, raw materials, semi-finished shoe or clothes products have occupied the whole exhibition hall. The projector on the wall redisplays the bustling working scenes of migrant workers through videos. The "birth and development" exhibition hall on the second floor tells the history of migrant workers over the past century in a chronological way. The term "migrant worker" first appeared in an exhibit here—the first issue of *Sociological Communication* in 1984. Inside the hall, there was also a reproduction of a green train travelled from Chengdu to Guangzhou. Its four windows review the inner scene in the past through videos.

The " Approaching hundreds of millions of migrant workers" exhibition hall on the third floor and fourth floor reappears all aspects of migrant workers' lives through helmets, BP machines, love letters, telephone cards and other objects.

After the tour on the fourth floor, visitors can also choose to role play as decorating workers, attendants, water courier, cleaner and take pictures through computers on the interactive platform set up by the museum. Besides, photos can be sent to their mailbox through the network after the unique experience. The museum is designed to pay tribute to millions of migrant workers for their immeasurable contribution to the development and modernization of Guangdong. Through recording and looking back into these historical footprints, it aims to remind city dwellers of those migrant workers and to befriend with them. "I came to Guangzhou ten years ago. I experienced the blossom of the dream after hardship. I am deeply touched by the humanistic care the museum assumes walking from the first floor to the fourth floor. It fully recognised the significance of being of those migrant workers as individuals and as a group", Huang Jianfeng, a migrant worker and poet said.

" China Mobile Population Development Report" issued by the Floating Population Service&Management Division of National Population and Family Planning Commission shows that 78.7% of the floating population are agricultural households, mainly young and middle-aged labour; children below 14 accounted for 20.8%; men accounted for 50.4% and women accounted for 49.6%. The average size of a floating family is 2.3 members; Among the population aged 16 to 59, 86. 8% received junior high school education and earns a monthly income of 1942 yuan on average. The data also shows that the Chinese floating population stays in the areas they are dwelling for usually more than five years. The average age of the floating population is 27.3 years old. This shows that most of the mobile population are at their most energetic and most active thinking age——"Golden Decade". They are able to advance learning and continue further study. Guangdong provincial government has been helping them

▲ In December 2010, the Guangdong Communist Youth League Provincial Committee tied up with Peking University and other related institutions to start the "Peking University Dream Come True Plan 100" project. It listed out 100 excellent candidates from 2501 migrant workers of the new generation and funded them fully in pursuing the Peking University online distant education undergraduate degree.

with personal development and "upward flowing" from the aspect of government policy these years. Individuals and groups from all walks of life roll out more and more incentive measures to motivate floating labours and help them advance in their career and life.

In December 2010, the Guangdong Communist Youth League Provincial Committee tied up with Peking University and other related institutions to start the "Peking University Dream Come True Plan 100" project. It listed out 100 excellent candidates from 2501 migrant workers of the new generation and funded them fully in pursuing the Peking University online distant education undergraduate degree.

Young man Pan Yan was born in a peasant family in Hubei. Pan Yan recalled his family was very poor and the whole memory about his childhood was hoeing the farmland, planting seeds and harvesting crops as well as irrigation and fertilisation. Acres of farmland were the only source of family income. His parents worked day and night, but couldn't make ends meet. As in the year of floods and droughts, not a single grain was reaped. The family had nothing to eat and had to borrow money from relatives or neighbours. Otherwise, they weren't able to make a living. Pan Yan, who determined to change his destiny through knowledge, had no choice but enrolled in a technical secondary school after graduating from junior high school, considering the family situation. He hoped to get a diploma after two years, by which time he can obtain skills and work to support the family. The year when he graduated, the government issued a new policy that technical secondary school students can also participate in college entrance examination. Pan Yan finally achieved his dream and got admission to a college in Wuhan. He was in second place in that entrance examination in his school. With help of friends and the family, Pan Yan pooled money needed for the first year's tuition fee and went to college successfully.

During the university time, almost all the summer and winter vacation, Pan Yan was doing part-time jobs. He worked as a network man in an internet bar and a worker at a construction site. The most impressive one was that during one summer vacation, he was doing odd jobs in a power supply station. It was nearly 40 degrees celcius every day. He carried heavy cables and climbed from one tower to another for only 20 yuan wages per day. The cable was thick and heavy, but there was no machine. All the cables were carried by labor from one tower to another. He felt sore and ache all over every day and he had got blisters on his feet and hands from the rubbing. Green injuries were added to old wounds. He felt keenly that his energy fell short of his intention and work efficiency went low. One day, foreman saw this and roared: "Would you quicken up? If you can't, stop coming tomorrow! Stop getting trouble! " He made it to the end of vacation finally. At the second semester of sophomore, Pan Yan went to the development zone to interview an IT intern position. His professional knowledge and skill about the computer are not bad as it was what he learned at the technical secondary school and his major at collge and he was successfully admitted. He went to work two days a week and earned 60 yuan per day. From then on, he no longer asked money from his parents.

In 2006, Pan Yan came to Shenzhen to work as an engineer in a foreign language training institution. In his spare time, he kept learning and finally got the Cisco certification in 2008. The following year, he got the Microsoft certification. Subsequently, he was promoted to supervisor and then to the IT manager in charge of Southern China. In the highly competitive Shenzhen labour market where talents gather, junior college degree still weighed on him. In early 2011, he read from newspaper that the "Peking University Dream Come True Plan 100" implemented by the Guangdong Communist Youth League Provincial Committee, which funds the new generation of industrial workers in pursuing undergraduate study. He went ecstacy. He applied online and confirmed his application on site. His reviewing work and preparation finally paid off and he became a member of the " Dream Come True Plan " .

Pan Yan successfully passed the unified English and computer examinations of the"Dream Come True Plan"as well as the English test for diploma in Beijing. His graduation thesis also reached standard of applying for the degree. In April, 2015, Pan Yan hopped to an enterprise through headhunting company and earned an annual income of 300,000 Yuan.

From the pilot scheme " Peking University 100" in 2010 to the widespread promotion of "Dream Come True Plan 100" in 2011, and then to blooming of the current new generation of sixty thousand industrial workers, "Dream Come True Plan" project keeps moving forward and its scale, to a certain degree, came close to that of a university. By 2016, it is the fourth year of holding the backbone trainee exchange camp of Dream Plan and the total trainees it cultivates in Guangdong come up to 8,000 at the end of 2016.

No Longer be a
Left Behind Child

The current estimation suggests that more than 61 million children are growing up in the Chinese countryside while their parents live and work elsewhere. Accompanying China's economic upheaval is the cost of the social dislocation of at least one generation of left behind children. Reuniting with their parents is their most simple but unreachable desire. To make the children no longer be left behind is to reunite them with their parents. Shall parents return home, or shall the children move with parents? Scholar Duan Chengrong's proposal is to adjust the social welfare system to enable children to follow their parents into cities.

2016 is the first year Guangdong province allows children of migrant workers to participate into college entrance exams locally. A total of 9,500 children of migrant workers whose household registration are not in Guangdong went in for the college entrance examination in Guangdong, among which, 1,056 children of migrant workers took the lead in Guangzhou. In the evening of June 6, 2016, after dinner, Han Junru got on her father's car and went back to Wei Ming Experimental School of Affiliated High School of Peking University. The Hans came to Guangzhou 14 years ago from Linyi, Shandong Prorince. Over the past 14 yeas, they have long before been adapted to the Guangzhou diet. Especially Han Junru, who followed her parents south at the age of four or five, has been brought up to a typical Cantonese. After living in Guangzhou for many years, Mrs. Han has gone native—specialised in cooking soups. Tonight's Chinese date and black-bone chicken soup was her daughter's favourite. "Without the college entrance examination reform, my family would have moved back to Linyi. I would by no means let my daughter become a left behind child." Han said. He is doing textile business in Guangzhou. After more than 10 years of hard work, he now has a happy family with one son & one daughter as well as a house and a car in Guangzhou. Yet, the issue of her daughter's college entrance examination still lingers in his mind before December 2015. When his daughter graduated from junior high school, the couple went back to Shangdong and took the child to meet Mr. Han's headteacher at his junior high school. "The matter we talked about most was our daughter's education. At that time, Guangdong adopted still the independent examination designing policy and test paper are different from that of Shangdong. We were worried and concerned with potential changes although Guangdong rolled out a new policy to enable children of migrant workers to sit college entrance examination locally. The teacher's suggestion is that she attends senior high school in Shangdong." Han said. The same matter also lingered on Zhang's heart, who came to Guangzhou in 1997 from Liuzhou, Guangxi. He gave up his job at a state-owned company and beat his own path in Guangzhou with his wife. Their daughter Zhang Qimeng was born in Guangzhou in 1998, a native-born Cantonese. Qimeng had great difficulty in getting into the Guangzhou education system as her parents' household registration are not in Guangzhou. In

2010, Qimeng managed to get admitted into The Affiliated Tianhe School of Guangdong Experimental Middle School. "We were in an invidious position of having to choose whether to let the child get the education at home. If we sent the child back to Guangxi under the care of her grandparents and participate in college entrance examination in Guangxi, we would save a great deal of money as well." Zhang said. However, both Han and Zhang determined to let the children get the education in Guangzhou. " We can't let our children be left behind children", they shared a common view. "If our daughter went back to Shandong, her mother would be sure to accompany her. A family can not be isolated for a long time. In that case, perhaps after a couple of years, I would close my business in Guangzhou and restart business in Linqi as well." Han said.

Both Han Junru and Zhang Qimeng attended boarding school. They went back home every weekend. Coincidentally, each of them has a nine-year-old younger brother. The night before the college entrance examination, Junru switched on TV unexpectedly. To relieve daughter's pressure, Han downloaded the film Utopia in the iPad for her. Both of their younger brothers are very thoughtful and considerate. Every time Junru being home, her younger brother never clamoured to watch TV or he would read books and do homework quietly by the side or play games in his own room lest he disturbs his sister. "I hope that there will be more children of migrant workers in the future to benefit from the college entrance examination reform and to enjoy equal opportunities as those local children. Especially these years, children of migrant workers are experiencing great competition in attending public senior high school. I hope my younger son can be a beneficiary during his entrance examinations for senior high school and college." Han said.

In Guangzhou, the education of children of migrant workers has been a heated issue. According to statistics, there were already 230,000 children of migrant workers who do not have Guangzhou's household registration studying in public schools in 2013, accounting for 42% of the students who do not have Guangzhou's household registration. In September 2016, the Municipal Government Executive Meeting discussed and approved the " Implementing Suggestions Concerning Further Strengthening the work of Compulsory Education for Children Living with Migrant Workers in Guangzhou" which clearly states that anyone who holds "Guangdong residence permit" which is applied in Guangzhou over one year can apply for compulsory education locally for his or her children based on accumulated evaluating credits. Strong in education, Yuexiu District brought it up in this program that preschool children of migrant workers who meet the standard enjoy the same rights of attending public kindergarten by lottery system as local children. Children of qualified migrant workers are also able to get the free compulsory education at Yuexiu's public primary schools. Panyu District proposed, starting from 2016, more free education quotas will be provided by allying with private schools; by 2020, children living with migrant workers in the district are expected to enjoy the same compulsory education rights as children registered locally. At the same time, the district advocates private schools to develop normatively, sustainably and excellently with specialties and urges them to provide more colourful choices for children living with migrant workers.

In Shenzhen, the survey of satisfaction towards compulsory education in 2015 showed that parents of non-Shenzhen household registration students gave higher scores than parents of Shenzhen household registration students. Shenzhen Municipal Education Bureau officer acclaimed that it indicates that Shenzhen puts public schools into full play concerning the issue of education of migrant workers' children. The fairness and balance over compulsory education in Shenzhen won recognition from parents. Among the 254,000 students enrolled in the compulsory education in Shenzhen in 2014, a total of 177,000 are non-Shenzhen household registered students, accounting for 69.7% of the total, and freshmen of non-Shenzhen household registration at both primary school and junior high school reach over 60% of the total. This ratio embodies that Shenzhen, as a first-tier city, maintains openness and fairness to the greatest degree over the issue of education of migrant workers' children. As a cosmopolitan with a large number of migrant workers, Shenzhen first in the country implemented the education registration system based on accumulated evaluating credits to guarantee migrant children' s education needs. According to the "1+5" policy, 6 to 15-year-old children whose household registration are not in Shenzhen, with the capability to learn, while their parents live in Shenzhen continuously for one consecutive year (either residential permit, social security, real estate license or residential place lease contract is valid for over one year) can apply for compulsory education in Shenzhen. One officer at Shenzhen Municipal Education Bureau expressed that the concept of the household registration system is fading gradually by the country. The accumulated evaluating credits-based education registration system aims to entitle children of migrant workers to enjoy equal education rights as local children.

I am Feeling
Good for
Being Here

Esther Haubensack: Famous Foreign Daughter-in-Law in Guangzhou

On July 2016, more than 3,000 episodes of the most popular sitcom in Guangdong, *Non-native Daughters-in-Law with*

Native sons, were broadcast. In the history of Chinese Television, 61

it enjoys the title of the longest broadcast, the largest number of episodes, the highest rating among sitcoms-alike broadcasting at the same time, the most comprehensive influence and the best economic effects. *Non-native*

Daughters-in-Law with Native Sons describes the funny stories occured to the Kang's family where four sons married four wifes from utterly

▲ *Non-native Daughters-in-Law with Native Sons* describes the funny stories occured to the Kang's family where four sons married four wifes from utterly different places and resulted in a series of hilarious scenes due to different life habits and culture backgrounds in Changsheng street, the old urban of Guangzhou.

different places and resulted in a series of hilarious scenes due to different life habits and culture backgrounds in Changsheng street, the old urban of Guangzhou.

In the sitcom, Esther Haubensack portrays "Diana", the wife of the fourth son of the Kangs, an English teacher in a private middle school in Guangdong. The pretty daughter-in-law from America is well-known in Changsheng street. Diana is well educated, simple and straightforward. She also sticks to principle strickly and takes everything seriously. She offers to take part in the family affairs and street public welfare matters while, because of cultural differences, sometimes she finds it hard to reach an agreement with her husband, mother-in-law or sister-in-law on some issues. She is typically stubborn and observes principles. To some extent, Diana's story is a true portrayal of the actress Hao Lianlu. Hao Lianlu is Esther Haubensack's Chinese name. She is from Germany and well- educated. She is a well-known foreigner in Guangzhou for starring in the sitcom *Non-native Daughters-in-Law with Native Sons*.

Hao Lianlu was born in a family of intellectuals in Munich, Germany and graduated from Ludwig Maximilian University of Munich with a master's degree in Sinology, and studied Chinese at Peking University for 1.5 years with full scholarship in 1992. By the end of 1993, the famous crosstalk artist Ding Guangquan had one sketch work that needed one foreign actress. Then, a teacher in Peking University recommended her to Ding. After meeting, master Ding thought that Hao Lianlu showed a talent for comedy and was not afraid of being on stage. Ding was quite satisfied with Hao Lianlu and agreed to have Hao starring the role immediately. Besides, Ding accepted Hao as a disciple. Correspondingly, Hao became a junior fellow disciple of Canadian "Da Shan", another famous comedy actor in China. She has won first prize in the Talent Contest for Foreigners in China and participated in large-scale theatrical performances hosted by CCTV many times. Her sketches like *foreign*

accents, racing to get a son-in-law, Rickshaw Boy and other pieces were gone viral. Besides, she has also hosted programs on the Central Television, Guangdong TV, and Macao TV and starred in the *Non*

native Daughters-in-Law with Native Sons, Ruan Aiguo in Hong Kong and many other films and television dramas. She is the most famous

comedy actress among foreigners in China. In Peking University, Hao Lianlu met a native Beijinger Wang Hongye. In early 1995, the two held a wedding. Later, considering career development, Hao Lianlu chose to go south alone to Guangdong to host a tour program. Soon she became starring in *Non-native Daughters-in-Law with Native Sons* as she speaks Cantonese fluently though with foreign accent. Her husband remains in Beijing. A few years later, Wang Hongye came to Guangzhou, following his wife. Since then, this pair of "foreign daughter-in-law and native Beijinger", has become neighborhood permanently living in Taojin street of Guangzhou.

Hao Lianlu is a typical German, very stubborn. Peng Xinzhi, starring the third son of Kangs, said Hao Lianlu is a typical German. Everything is well in order for her. "You know instantly if you look at her car, very neat."

In addition, Hao Lianlu is quite faithful to the script. "We often discuss the script with each other and then play the drama rather than stick to script 100%. But she is not used to this. She must follow the script. But gradually, she was influenced by us and learned to be more flexible."

Non-native Daughters-in-Law with Native Sons was on premiere in November 2000, which has been broadcast for nearly 17 years. Hao Lianlu didn't show up a lot in the sitcom. She can not remember when her last filming was, neither does she

▲ What worth observing is that Hao, as a graduate of Peking University with a master's degree in Sinology, is now a full-time wife and she educates her two children at home. She thinks differently towards current education in China. She was amazed and felt incredible when she learned some college graduates even can not switch light bulbs.

know when the next play will be. Everything is at the disposal of the sitcom crew. Although in the play, Diana is very vigorous and active, in reality, Hao Lianlu is a quiet person. One director in a TV channel in Guangzhou recalled that it was usually noisy at the scene and everyone was occupied with their own matters while tall Hao Lianlu liked crouching at the corner and reading quietly. Regardless the noisy environment, she didn't even bother to lift her head. During the most popular time of *Non-native Daughters-in-Law with Native Sons*, Han Lianlu received a variety of invitations to shoot films, attending shows and hosting activities, but few of them were brought up by her first. Generally, it was others that come to her. "If somebody invites me, then I accept; If no one invites me, I would not bother. Playing in the film is troublesome. So it is when there is no play." She is not so ambitious about filming, to which her attitude is at pleasure.

What worth observing is that Hao, as a graduate of Peking University with a master's degree in Sinology, is now a full-time wife and she educates her two children at home. She thinks differently towards current education in China. She was amazed and felt incredible when she learned some college graduates even can not switch light bulbs.

She also visited domestic schools but she did not approve the way children were educated there. In her view, a teacher, with forty or fifty students ih his/her class, can rarely communicate with their parents. The child remains at school at least eight hours a day. Except for the time for homework and sleep, children rarely have time to communicate with their parents. Thus parents know nothing about what the children learned, said and thought in school. That doesn't work. Therefore, Hao Lianlu's two children did not go to school, but stayed at home and were educated by their mother. There is nothing special about Hao's education methods, who graduated from the Peking University and got the advanced education from Germany. She communicates with the children, introduces them the background and contents of the textbooks. She advises them to learn in life and learn from crafts, to which Hao's parents-in-law finds it hard to comprehend. In China, many parents spare no efforts sending their children to a key school and even spend millions of yuan trying to buy a house in the vicinity of the public school, which is excellent in public's eyes. This foreign daughter-in-law insisted on teaching children at home despite they can absolutely afford a good school. On this matter, Hao's stubborn character was exposed again. It's her call. "From 8 am to 5 pm, the children were circled together and instilled with ideas and knowledge. All the teacher teaches is that they shall look at issues in this way or that perspective. The children can get high marks as long as they behave well. They have no time to question and to doubt for the truth. After school, they are totally blank and are in a mess. Hundreds of years ago, there is no school when everyone is learning at home. Why is it not suitable now? This is a new era when we need brainstorming. Something that you feel wrong is probably the mainstream in other culture or times. "Hao was so stubborn that her parents-in-law can only shrug and let it go.

After living in Guangzhou for more than a decade, Hao Lianlu has been fully immersed into the city. She is concerned about the development of Guangzhou. When Guangzhou advocated the implementation of garbage classification, Hao Lianlu accepted media's interview and shared her experience of sorting out the garbage. "My friends often complain that they have a mound of garbage every day. I would then tell them' if you can sort out the part which is not necessarily be disposed of and recycle them, then the garbage left is not much.'" According to Hao Lianlu, she would sort the bathroom garbage, plastic products, and glass bottles out separately. In addition, she would flatten the paper waste and stack them together.

These categorized garbages would be stored in the kitchen before she called on someone to collect them when it accumulated to a certain amount. Then the rest was a small amount of garbage produced in the kitchen, over which Hao Lianlu sighed most. "It seems useless. Actually, in Germany, almost everyone has a small garden where these precious organic wastes are good fertilizer. What a pity that they can only be disposed of in Guangzhou."

Matt: Foreign Son-in Law in Guangzhou

Every time British Matt meets a new Chinese friend, he would introduce himself in Chinese enthusiastically and pronounce every Chinese word clearly with full tone effortlessly, "Ni Hao, Wo Jiao Ma te". But when you expect him to chat with you further in fluent Chinese, you are doomed to be disappointed as it is almost the only Chinese that he could say. Despite that this burly handsome British man has been living in China for nine years and teaches English in the kindergarten, it turns out he fails to speak Chinese by any means.

Many people were surprised as they learned that Matt is a kindergarten teacher. In fact, Matt is more like a plane model, fitness coach, or corporate executive. He is as burly as a solemn ancient Greek sculpture. His deep eye socket, high nose, decent dress highlights his British gentleman's temperament. But in the opinions of those who are familiar with Matt, kindergarten teacher suits him best. He is kind and humorous with colorful facial expressions. Besides, he can imitate others so vividly to perfection. The unique sense of humor of British makes him pleasing and popular. Even if others fail to comprehend the laughing points in his words, they are amused by his animated expression.

Before coming to China, Matt was a purchaser at a British

construction company, responsible for purchasing raw materials for interior decorations. During the 2008 economic crisis, Britain also got stuck in great recession and most people faced unemployment. Matt was no exception. Overwhelmed by the torrent of unemployment, he felt impotent more than frustrated. Matt attributed it to the economic condition rather than his ability. He felt he could not pull himself together instantly and get reemployment. So, the exhausted Matt decided to take a break and have a long holiday. Instead of dining and traveling, he hoped to pick up something meaningful and something he was really into. Once, Matt discovered a volunteer activity to teach English in a small village in China by chance. In the mysterious oriental country, in a quiet mountain village, innocent children are smiling. Matt sketched the picture in his mind. "Isn't it exactly what I want?" He felt a sudden impulsion and excitedly enrolled in this six-weeks volunteer event and then came to China. It is just that he did not expect his own life embraced an about-face thoroughly. His fate with China turned out to be more than six weeks, but nine years or longer.

Matt and his friends came to Yangshuo County, Guilin City of Guangxi Province. In the year of the reign of Nan Song Emperor Zhaokuo (AD 1201), Wang Zhenggong, Criminal Prison Officer at Guangnanxilu (current Guangxi province), indited a poem: "The mountains and rivers in Guilin are the finest under the heaven, you can meditate the true meaning of the mountains and the rivers here." Since then, "Guilin Scenery, Finest under Heaven" has become China's best-known tourism advertisement worldwide. Guilin, as one of China's earliest open tourism cities, is also one of the five cities(Beijing, Xi'an, Shanghai, Guilin, Guangzhou), which earliestly hosted foreign tourists, and began hosting foreign heads of state as early as 1972. Over the past 40 years, Guilin not only became a well-known tourist destination for foreigners, but its number of foreign tourists visited also ranked the forefront of that of national prefecture-level cities. West Street, the oldest street in Yangshuo County, was dubbed "the Largest English Corner" in China. Every year, foreigners traveling or living here are equivalent to three times of the number of the natives.

As time went by, the newly arrival's misunderstanding was quickly thrown off. And they were often invited to the local villagers' home in the evening. Regardless of the language barrier, they sat together and communicated through body language or painting. The children's favorite thing was to ask the four foreign teachers a variety of questions. Holding books, they pointed at the British map in the picture, "Are you from there?", their innocent eyes filled with curiosity. Matt was touched. " It seems nice to be a teacher!" The seed of being a teacher was rooted in Matt's heart.

After six weeks of volunteer activity, Matt was not willing to leave. On the Tuesday he was supposed to arrive in England, he had a phone call with his friends: "I do not go back and I decided to stay in China."

"Are you crazy? You have nothing in China!"

"Similarly, there is nothing appealing in Britain that deserves me returning, either."

Matt remained in China. With the help of the project leader, he came to Guangzhou. It was a sunny day when he arrived in Guangzhou on that Sunday. While he was amazed at the fragrant sweet osmanthus trees and clear river in Yangshuo, he was half familiar and half odd with Guangzhou, a metropolis, where everything can be eaten, bought and observed. As long as he can find a job, he can live better off in Guangzhou as he was in England. The next morning, he was informed to be interviewed as an English teacher at a kindergarten, and successfully he got the job. Nine years passed and he is still doing the job. Matt's mother is a teacher. She had asked Matt and his brother whether they wanted to be a teacher as her when Matt was 18 years old. By that time, they both refused their mother's proposal with curt finality, to which his mother even felt a sense of loss. However, as if fate is manipulating, Matt ran away at the corner of fate, only to appear on the threshold of a career as a teacher without any signs, by which carrying out his mom's wish. What is more interesting is that Matt's brother is also an English teacher in Australia.

The first friend he got to know in Guangzhou was a girl who became his wife later. After three days of his arrival, he passed the old site of Guangzhou Library and found a group of people gathered on the square. There were both Chinese and foreigners. His curiosity was piqued and he came forward and found it was an "English corner." Since the 1990s, three kinds of oral English activities began to show up in Chinese cities, namely, English Corner, English Salon and English Party. In Guangzhou, there are four English Corners and the old site of Guangzhou library is one of them. Every Sunday morning, in the open space in front of the banyan tree of a hundred years old, English lovers get together and they exchange ideas and opinions in English. Some people remark that "English Corner" in China is also a marriage agency, through which many beautiful love stories get started. Matt confirmed its certainty with his own experience. That day, a sweet girl came forward towards Matt. Two people greeted each other. In a few words later, they found a place to sit down and began chatting freely. As for the contents, Matt couldn't recall much but he was pleased with the whole time. Two young people growing in distinct environment happened to share a lot of interests in common and both became curious about the other's life. They had a pleasant time that morning as if they felt an affinity towards each other at first sight. Matt was almost drowned in the girl's sweet smiling. He was delighted to meet this charming girl by chance. Matt asked the girl's contact politely but was rejected. "Well, it is natural for Chinese to be prudent and implicit." Matt was not discouraged. They appointed to meet each other at the English Corner next time. After several meetings, the two became friends. She helped Matt look for a house and took him to hang around Guangzhou. They often met and had meals together. Surely, Matt managed to get that girl's phone number. The two fell in love with each other soon and eventually got married.

In Matt's opinion, sometimes her wife is as cute as a child. In other times, she is elegant, independent as well as capable.She would be excited for a while as she learned how to cook a dish. Meanwhile, he is concerned with her as she lives under too much pressure. She would never complain about her excessive workload to her boss. Matt's wife works in an English language training center. At first, she was a secretary. Later her boss found that her English is pretty good and assigned her to be an English teacher. Soon after that, her boss found she is also adroit at computer so she was assigned to teach computer too. The job duty was determined by the boss without considering her opinions. In addition to her own duty, she has to do a lot of other things, many of which go beyond the scope of her job duty. In the UK, if a staff feels that the boss makes unreasonable requests, they would bring it up and negotiate with the boss. While in China, most staffs are obedient and dare not to speak out their dissatisfaction. Matt holds that it is because there is too much competition in the country due to a large population. Matt has persuaded his wife to say "no" many times. Yet, though his wife complains about it orally, she still shows great assiduity in all her work. As time passed by, Matt got used to it and began to understand the difficulties. He shows more comprehension and support when his wife moans occasionally and tries to relieve her grievance.

Chinese women's thrifty virtue is highly exalted. While, in Matt's view, they are being too strict on themselves. Matt's wife always hesitates to buy those expensive things that appeal to her. Matt thinks buying favorite thing is a great matter, so he would persuade her to buy it, even more solicitously than the salesperson. In most cases, his wife still chose to walk away. There were several times when Matt secretly bought them back as gifts, she would blame that he was wasting money, but still could not help smiling joyfully. Matt always brainwashes his wife: "What matters is that you like it not money!"

Matt has been living in Guangzhou for nine years. Yet, he still cannot speak fluent Chinese. When he first came to Guangzhou, he also went to a Chinese class, but eventually, he gave up. Matt didn't owe it to his own problem but to what taught by the Chinese class was not what he really wanted. Matt hoped to learn more daily expression like how to call a taxi, how to communicate in Chinese at a bank. Teachers at the Chinese school seemed to prefer imparting fixed knowledge like "bpmf" (Chinese consonant). Matt found it boring although he recognized that he should start from the basics. He did not intend to spend so much time learning how to speak every word with full tone and with accurate syntax. A lot of foreigners went to England, without learning English systematically. Yet, they live well in England for decades. Luckily, the fact that he cannot speak Chinese does not have much influence on Matt's life. In Guangzhou,

▲ Now, Matt and his wife have a five-year-old boy named Austin. The kinship runs through between this British man and China.

generally, people of any age can speak a little bit English. For example, most waiters in restaurants can speak English and they won't show confusion if Matt orders in English. He can also call a taxi in English. In the case when a driver takes a detour, he would warn, "Hey, friend, you seemed deviate from the original path. I actually know the route!" He even thinks that it is easier to learn Cantonese than Mandarin. Cantonese has nine different tones, and it sounds like singing when you speak Cantonese. It is rhythmic. Although there are not strong motives and perseverance for Matt to learn Chinese, it still sticks in his throat as his wife always mocks him on this matter relentlessly. In order to prove himself, he once had wanted to indulge himself in pure Chinese language environment in a small city in China for a couple of years so that he can show up with fluent Chinese in front of his wife after return.

Now, Matt and his wife have a five-year-old boy named Austin. The kinship runs through between this British man and China. The villain never sits still. Even in the heavy rainy days, he hopes to play outside. Perhaps having inherited the body features of British, when his Chinese classmates are wearing coats, he only wears a T-shirt. It makes Matt and his wife feel troublesome and they make great efforts to manage to have him wear more clothes. As the old saying goes, Austin is like "the blue from indigo plant which is deeper than its origin." Compared with Matt who could not learn to speak Chinese, Austin's talent for language is way too better. At an early age, he can speak Mandarin, Cantonese, and English and switch language effortlessly among kindergarten, his grandmother, mom, and dad.

Like Hao Lianlu, Matt also formed his own thoughts on Chinese education. Most parents are extremely deferential to him, which makes him feel ill-at-ease. At Chinese schools, a teacher is more a boss than a teacher. As for meetings at Chinese schools, he feels parents are more likely to just sit down and listen carefully to what the teacher says, while the teacher makes comments on every student, even their parents. "You are good on this but you did wrong on that. Be careful not to commit it again." Parents just nod in a silence until the teacher finishes his speech. Then the meeting is dismissed. As a foreigner, he actually wants to change this situation and discusses it freely with parents at meetings on how to make students or the school be better, rather than that parents follow blindly what the teacher says. However, the expected effects are not achieved. Like in a party, the director keeps trying to create an ambiance of liveness while the audience responds with apathy or even just viewing the director's efforts as a solo. As time went by, Matt did not urge for change anymore and once again he attributed this to the difference of culture. In China, both parents and students are obedient. To be a teacher is to be authoritative. If a student behaves badly, you just tell him "I might want to talk to your parents." and then the student turns obedient immediately. In the UK, the students will call their mother by themselves and inform their mother "Our teacher wants to talk to you." After passing the phone to the teacher, they would continue the game they were playing.

It's not surprising that a British who lived and worked in London for many years said that he loves the weather and food in Guangzhou. Matt made great efforts to keep fit since living in Guangzhou. Faced with a variety of dishes, he can either eat less or work out more after eating. Matt could not resist the temptation of delicious food and jumped to the latter. He is willing to pay his dues for food and fitness. In the UK, Matt is troubled by nothing inviting to eat. In Guangzhou, his trouble goes to another end. He has difficulty in picking what to eat.He is obsessed with, not just local Cantonese cuisine, but delicious food from all over the world in Guangzhou. But like many other foreigners, Matt has a blacklist of food as well. The chicken claws preferred by local people, however, frighten Matt. Once on a train, for the first time, he saw someone eating chicken claws. One boy, sitting on the opposite seat, was so preoccupied in eating the chicken claws as if everything around was of no significance except the chicken claws. Matt looked blankly for a long time and the boy's satisfied expression left a deep impression on him.Under his wife's compulsion, Matt tried chicken claws once. The strange tendons and bones, as well as the unprecedented taste, made him swear never to eat them again. Interestingly, his son, Austin particularly likes to eat chicken claws. Once, Matt took his wife and Austin back to England. At a gathering, Austin suddenly talked to his mom: "I want to eat chicken claws!" People around were all surprised and stared at him as if looking at a small monster. Matt found it particularly fun that the collision of Chinese and Western food culture assumed in such a dramatic and vivid way.

Today's Matt has been fully integrated into the life of Guangzhou and has become an ordinary resident in the neighborhood. He likes to gather with friends at night to enjoy food or take a walk after dinner in cool or warm weather. He feels cozy living here. One of the great pleasures of his life is to watch the weather forecast of his hometown in the UK, and then post the screenshots of weather forecasts of Guangzhou and his hometown on the social network and joked: "lol, What a pity! It looks so cold there. I only wear two clothes in winter here."

Matt celebrates every "foreign festival" as well as traditional Chinese festivals. At Christmas, Matt is the most popular person in kindergarten because he would dress up as Santa Claus and bring gifts to the kids in kindergarten. Some children can recognize Matt sharply. They are so excited that they climb on Matt's shoulder and pull his beard, giggling and screaming. As for Chinese Spring Festival, Matt is not so enthusiastic. The annual Spring Festival travel season——Chunyun makes Matt feel amazing and unbelievable. People like migratory birds, flock to airports, railway stations, bus stations before Chinese Lunar New Year day. Within a few days, a city is almost empty. A week later, the city is intensely populated again. Matt also hopes to be a member of migration team during the Spring Festival. For him, an ideal Spring Festival holiday is to visit his younger brother in Australia and enjoy the sunny beach in the southern hemisphere. Most of the years, he simply accompanied his wife to celebrate Spring Festival with relatives in Guangzhou. The reunion at Chinese Lunar New Year makes Matt realize the significance of family for Chinese people. However, he seems somewhat lonely in the lively atmosphere when dozens of people chat in Chinese and his wife has no time to interpret for him. Most of the time, Mark has nothing to do but laughs by the side. The children are always hilarious to see Matt and demand playing with Matt. As a result, Matt has to continue playing the role of leader among kids.

Guangzhou has been ranked as one of the most livable cities in China. Sometimes, she is like a lady, ready to make a debut shining with deep and vivid tints. Sometimes, she is as graceful as a pretty middle-class girl, waiting for someone else to explore her beauty. Brimming with vitality and livingness, Guangzhou is a megacity where various people lead a colorful and distinct life and seek their own happiness. It is more the people living in the city than the city itself that appeals to Matt. He described people in some of the big cities he had ever been to as restless and adrift. People there are always making a bustle in making money. Even if you greeted "hello" enthusiastically in front of them, few people would cast an eye on you. In contrast, Guangzhou residents are temperate and hospitable. Because of them, Guangzhou is a city brimming with warmth.

Matt still misses Britain sometimes. Every year, he goes back to Britain to spend time with friends and his family in Britain twice. But if it is to be a long time, he feels boring instead. The man, who has been accustomed to Guangzhou weather, yet, fails to adapt to the British climate. In the cold winter, he just sits inside the house and shivers, staring at the raindrops. The social network also makes him feel estranged from old friends. Few new topics can be shared. For example, house decoration or purchase of a new car, which are mostly talked by his old friends during meeting, are already shown on their social network. Matt has seen them already, therefore, there is nothing new.

In 2015, Matt returned to Yangshuo, the small village he stayed seven years ago, on a bullet train. It is the first land he stepped on in China, also the place where he fell in love with China and decided to stay. Walking on the road he helped build, his light-colored pupils no longer caught people's attentions; People in the shopping mall do not stare at him with curiosity as before. Things have changed. The sight is renewed. The person may leave but the affection remains. If Yangshuo is the first love for Matt, then Guangzhou is the inseparable lifetime spouse. For nine years, Matt witnessed massive changes and developments of Guangzhou while Guangzhou also proved his adherence to his initial passion. The two of them long before have become inextricable.

▲ The Matts and Matt's students

Welcome Foreign Neighbors with Ready Service

Latest statistics from Guangzhou police show that the number of foreigners permanently living in Guangzhou is about 80,000 and the maximum can be up to nearly 120,000; the top five countries where those foreign residents come from are South Korea, Japan, the United States, India, and Canada. Hao Lianlu's and Matt's life are "the epitome of that of foreigners in Guangzhou." Nowadays, foreigners living in Guangzhou are usually located around a few areas as follow: the area of the Xiushan mansion, Taojin road, Garden hotel, the Jianshe Sixth road, Jianshe Main road, which surrounds the Huanshi East road. Most Africans dealing with trade and some European and Japanese consulates are based here;

The area of Tiyu East road, Tianhe road, Longkou West road, Linhezhong road, whose center is the Tianhe North road. Most Japanese, Americans, Europeans dealing with trade live here as a great number of foreign company offices are located in the CITIC Tower;

People from East Asian and Southeast Asian countries such as Japan, Thailand, and Malaysia mainly live in Qifu Cottage, and Lijiang Garden in the Panyu District, where a number of large-scale communites with well-equipped infrastructures lie.

The San Yuan Li area, such as the Jingui village and Airport road

▲ The foreigner has melted into local life.

community and other places. Mainly Africans who trade shoes and clothing gathered here. In recentl years, many Koreans engaged in trade between China and South Korea also congregated here.

Parkview Green Garden in Tianhe North road. Foreign households are mainly from Saudi Arabia, Iran, Turkey, Britain, Japan, South Korea and other countries respectively.

A majority of households in Tianxiu Building in Yuexiu District are Africans and Middle Eastern businessmen. Among the 600 offices in Tianxiu Building, 70% of which are rented by the Middle East businessmen and Africans. They sell daily necessities, clothing, shoes and hats, textiles, and even sewing machines, lanterns and other Chinese goods which are quite rare nowadays in China.

According to a survey by *Nanfang Daily*, among a rating of the impression of Guangzhou, the full point of which is 10, 42% of foreigners evaluated Guangzhou at 8 points plus. Most foreigners think that Guangzhou people are cool and behave casually towards foreigners. Chad from the United States said that the Beijinger is very hospitable towards foreigners, and even invite foreigners to have a meal at home; the Shanghai people will treat foreigners as trade targets and always hope to gain interests from foreigners. And in Jiujiang of Jiangxi, parents would encourage their kids to practice English with foreigners. In Guangzhou, when Chad follows the flow to get out of the subway, he feels that he is a citizen of Guangzhou, where people don't bother to cast too much attention on foreigners. "I think I can use the phrase 'don' t care' to describe Guangzhou people's attitude towards foreigners."

Though, people in Guangzhou don't pay much attention to foreigners, Guangzhou is an understated and pragamatic city while talk less and do more. The Guangzhou government is concerned with the lives of foreign residents. In recent years, Guangzhou government has been committed to improving services and managements for foreigners and tries to innovate in order to provide a more comfortable and cozy environment for foreigners in Guangzhou and offer conveniences for them as much as possible.

On June 14, 2013, the missing Russian girl Astafyeva Yulia finally met her mother after one month of no contact. Astafyeva Yulia came to China alone by train through Manchuria in March 2013. In June, she suddenly lost contact with her parents and her friends also went somewhere else. She was discovered without any money and identity card by people in a store in

Orange Tree village, Luopu subdistrict of Panyu, holding a pack of cigarettes and a bottle of water tightly. After receiving reports from the enthusiastic local residents, the police decided to send her to the rescue station in Panyu district for the moment and then brought her back to the management and service workstation for foreigners in Luopu subdistrict to figure out what happened. With the help of interpreters in the workstation, the police called Astafyeva Yulia 's mom and learned that Astafyeva Yulia suffered from epilepsy. Everything is fine when she is not sick and she had been in contact with the family until June 7. Her mom assumed that she had an attack of epilepsy and then immediately reported it to the Consulate. When Astafyeva Yulia 's mother flew to Guangzhou to pick up her daughter, she was very grateful to the staffs at the workstation and Panyu district. The Foreigners Service Station which rescued Astafyeva Yulia was established in 2008 and is the first of its kind set up in Guangzhou, aiming to provide management and services for foreigners. Any foreigners who wish to live in the Luoxi area, Panyu district, can complete all the necessary accommodation registration procedures in the vicinity without going far away to a distant police station. At the same time, the local police can also provide various necessary on-site services for foreigners living in the vicinity. At present, Foreign Service Workstations are being gradually set up in all subdistricts or towns where more than 200 foreigners reside, just like Luopu subdistrict.

With the official operation of Metro Line 6, 604 foreign residents choose to live in Jinsha subdistrict, Baiyun district of Guangzhou, where transportation is increasingly convenient. It's an increase by 91% while they are from more than 80 countries and areas, of which the majority are Asians and Africans. As more and more foreigners live here, local residents sometimes are concerned with problems brought on by cultural differences. For example, foreigners like to entertain with friends at home, while the local residents are relatively more into tranquil and peaceful life. In order to make foreign neighbors and local neighborhoods get along well with each other, Jinsha subdistrict neighborhood committee set up a Management and Service Workstation for foreigners living there and established a joint meeting mechanism which is led by police station, while attended by subdistrict office, neighborhood committees, property management companies and related functional departments to improve the efficiency

▲ More and more foreigners found their opportunities to achieve prosperity in Guangdong.

and response speed of dealing with foreigners- related issues and matters and thus realized the socialized management over foreigners. In addition, Jinsha subdistrict hires interpreters through social translation platforms to participate in the foreigners-related affairs in order to solve the problem of lacking interpretation manpower in daily work in the police station, which strengthens the idea of "all policeman being able to deal with foreign affairs". Guangzhou police produced Chinese and English version leaflets concerning foreign-related affairs and placed a touch-sensitive query machine in the service workstation for foreigners working in Guangzhou, which involves the profile of Jinsha subdistrict, accommodation registration process, guidance on registration of visa and other relevant information to facilitate foreigners to understand the relevant laws and regulations and the processing procedure. Jinsha subdistrict police station also opened a WeChat official account. Foreigners, landlords, real estate agencies, property management companies can receive all kinds of service information, kind warning, and other real-time information as long as they scan its QR code and follow the official account.

Located in Baohan area, Dengfeng subdistrict, Yuexiu district, the famous household "African village" is where one-fifth of the African residents in Guangzhou are living, amounting to more than 1,000 people. In the flush times, if all the African tourists, businessmen and short term visitors are taken into consideration, it can reach more than 10,000 people. In order to help foreigners living in Guangzhou solve their problems and get integrated into local life, community workers distributed over 200 questionnaires, visited from household to household and rolled out community integration program based on foreigners' needs. Associate Professor of Sociology at Guangzhou University and Guangzhou Social Work Development Center Director Wang Liang said, "The survey shows that their biggest problem is language learning. So our first step is to hold Chinese classes - 'Chinese Course', which lasts from 3 pm to 5 pm, from Monday to Saturday. In this way, they can master some Chinese in daily expression to help them see a doctor, change money, inquiry about the route, or even conduct simple business." At Chinese class, students from all over the world share their own stories and seek a sense of belonging and security, regardless of their status or background. Some foreigners who live in Guangzhou for a longer time who have a better command of Chinese language will volunteer during their spare time. These who have been served offer to volunteer for those newly-arrived foreigners. In order to achieve the service at "zero distance", Yuexiu district has also established an interactive internet platform for foreigners and made use of information collection equipment "Document Green Passage" to facilitate foreigners to apply for visa extensions or deal with other matters in the vicinity.

On June 30, 2016, the Special Council held by IOM(International Organization for Migration) adopted a resolution to approve China as a member of the IOM and began a new chapter in the cooperation between China and the IOM. Guangzhou, as a window to observe China' s management of foreign immigrants, was highly spoken of by the IOM for its innovative practices.

Since I am Here,
I am not Leaving

Ma Li'an: I have the Deepest Love for Shenzhen

Many people love shenzhen, but unlike most people who are fascinated by Shenzhen's constant changes, great vigour and strong momentum, there is one American woman who is especially interested in the history of Shenzhen and its urban villages. Some people say that Shenzhen is a "cultural desert", she plunged headlong into that "desert", and immersed herself in it for 22 years, only to discover a ubiquitous oasis hiding in the "desert". She would argue with anyone who remarked that Shenzhen is a city without culture. She is Ma Li' an, an anthropologist from the United States. She currently works at the Hong Kong Baptist University (Shenzhen) and mainly studies the historical changes of urban villages in Shenzhen. Where there are meetings, salons concerning the topic of urban villages, there is the presence of Ma.

" Where did you come from?""Where did you get married?""From which place did you go to the market?" From April to October 2015, Ma Li'an and her colleague Fu Na led a research team to dictate 15 old men' s oral history in Futian District, Shenzhen. Fifteen ordinary stories told by fifteen old men respectively composed the special memory of the city. Ma Li'an invited citizens of different ages to engage in making the "Futian stories" collected into illustrations. For six months, Ma Li' an and her team visited 15 villages in Futian District and had conversation style interview with the elderly people in those villages, during which she had many interesting findings. For example, there is no doubt that Shenzhen, as an international metropolis, is an immigrant city. In most people's views, labels like "in ternationalisation""immigration" are connected to Shenzhen after the reform and opening up. In fact, the migration can date back to the Song Dynasty. There are mainly 8 surnames in 15 villages of Futian District. Among them, ancestors of Huang migrated from Henan, passing through Fujian, Jiangxi and came to Xiasha, Shangmeilin, Shangsha and Futian. In Huanggang village and Shuiwei village, there are descendants of Wen Tianxiang and Zhuangzi. The influx of migrants from other parts of the country has drastically altered the city's linguistic landscape. At least seven vernaculars are observed. Xin'an county official mandarin dialect is spoken in Longgang and Bao'an, used by around 5,000 speakers. Hakka dialect is a relatively popular dialect. There is also Weitou dialect which is between Cantonese and Hakka dialect. Dapeng dialect was spoken among garrison in Da Peng Suo Town. The original inhabitants of Pingshan also speak Zhanmi dialect, which is transformed from Hakka dialect. Besides, Dan dialect was spoken by some fishers in the past. This is consistent with the history of Shenzhen being a fishing village before reform and opening up. Mandarin did not become the widely used language until the 1990s when numerous people from northern China migrated to Shenzhen. In the view of Ma Li'an, the internationalisation of Shenzhen was as early as in the 19th century when people in Futian village worshipped Mazu. Tianhou

Mazu Temple in Nanshan District has always been one important stop of the Maritime Silk Road. Zheng He passed here when he travelled to the west. In fact, the custom of worshipping Mazu is still prevailing in the coastal areas of Fujian, Zhejiang, Guangdong.Southerners migrated and carried with their faith in Mazu to China's Taiwan, Vietnam, Japan and Southeast Asia. Now, there are about 1,500 Mazu Temples in 26 countries.

As one of the activities of the 2015 International Urban Images Festival-Shenzhen(Futian), Ma Li'an initiated the activity " Futian Story: New Genealogy" at the Futian Library. In a press conference, Ma Li'an's Beijing accent left a profound impression on the media presented. She initiated the activity to inspire new generations to reflect on Shenzhen's history, understand the land below their feet and thus grow connections with the land. For example, they would ask a ten-year-old child to make out his/her own house in the picture, to speak his/her own dialect and tell people his/her family's history. The child got connected to time and space through reflection on the history. If the child goes to Japan, he/she will find there is Tianhou temple in Japan as in Shenzhen. There is no kinship between Japanese and Chinese. Neither do they speak the same language. Why do they all worship the Tianhou(Mazu)? The child will raise question like this. They prompt young generations to think about the history of the city, and their connection with the city, which is Ma's initial intention. The sense of belonging and the understanding of history towards the city can't be achieved through one lesson. It is a process, and what Ma is doing is planting the seeds.

As early as in the sixth grade during primary school, Ma Li'an has been connected to Shenzhen. Her school asked the children to make a report of the third world countries and her report focused on China. Since then, she became interested in this extraordinary country. In high school, Ma Li'an had an exchange experience in the Philippines for one year. Living at a local overseas Chinese's house, she got to know Chinese culture and language. At university, she learned Chinese in-depth in Taiwan, which laid a solid foundation for her Chinese capability. In 1994, Ma Li'an was studying in Houston and she received a delegation from Shenzhen, in that she could speak Chinese fluently. One member of the delegation mentioned he can introduce her to do anthropological research in the University of Shenzhen.

Shenzhen and Houston are sister cities, but Ma Li'an knew nothing about Shenzhen. This offer prompted Ma to refer to related documents about Shenzhen instantly. She learned roughly that the development strategy of Houston is quite similar to that of Shenzhen. Both cities possess harbour resources and large industrial projects. Houston mainly thrives on oil resources, which leads to great air pollution. Most cities focus on economic development prior to environment protection. She became curious about Shenzhen and wanted to see whether the city on the other side of the ocean followed the same path. In 1995, Ma Li'an set foot on the land of Shenzhen with her doctoral thesis research. Prior to this, she has been to Beijing, Shanghai, Guangzhou. In the United States, generally, people who are interested in Chinese or Sinology would prefer Beijing,

Shanghai and Guangzhou as well. While Ma Li'an was in Shenzhen, a lot of friends advised her to go to Beijing to do research. Ma Li'an then had one interesting finding, namely, in the past, people's pride of one city lies more on its history and culture rather than modernization. The view has a dramatic transition today. Now many people began to feel proud of Shenzhen, believing that it was a right decision to come to Shenzhen, though Shenzhen was not on most people's list at that time. A majority of people felt that Shenzhen was an economic city rather than cultural city and that culture was supposed to be in Beijing or Shanghai. Because of this, history and modernization had a splendid collision in Shenzhen. Shenzhen hopes to be a city of history and culture, but also an international metropolis like Hong Kong. It hopes to compound them together.

When Ma first arrived in Shenzhen, she lived in the international students' apartment of the University of Shenzhen with a monthly rent of $ 500. The expensive rental compelled her to look for another dwelling. Finally, she was exhilarated to find a room in Yuehaimen village near the university and moved in with a monthly rental of less than 600 yuan successfully. She settled down and began her interview and research. She has become an "Urban Village" resident and commenced her lifelong connection with "Urban Village".

Ma Li'an's love for the urban village is somewhat obstinate. Whenever she hears someone belittling the urban village as "dirty, messy, inferior and of low quality", she could not help standing out and defending it, "In the big city, it is almost impossible to find a cheap place which is 20 minutes' drive from the urban district. For most young people, they commence their career right from the urban village." In her view, urban village accounted for less than 5% of the total space of Shenzhen, but lived with more than half of the population. The urban village provides not only the living residences but also basic jobs like cleaner, barreled water bearer and so on. It enables migrants to pursue their dreams and change their living standards and identities. If they were not the second generation of wealthy people or officials, young people are bound to settle down in urban villages first. These people are not unpolished, uncultured, or unrefined. Neither are they the burden dragging Shenzhen's development. On the contrary, they are the hope of Shenzhen, and urban village is the place where dreams breed. If there were no urban villages providing cheap rentals, food and facilities, they would not be able to remain here and strive for their own future as well as the future of the city. Ultimately, those young people moved into the city center and skyscrapers and did well on their own efforts, thus they become decent Shenzheners. Ma Li'an has lived in the urban villages in Tianmian, Shazui and Nantoulaojie. She felt strongly that the existence of urban village made great contributions to the development of the city. Thus, she decided to explore Shenzhen based on the topic of urban village.

"The vigorousness is hidden more in urban villages like Baishizhou than high-end residential areas, in that those high-end residential areas are not the source of success, but a place to enjoy the fruits while the people living in urban villages are playing the role of reformer and destiny changer.

To a certain degree, treating them well preserves the vigorousness of the city." Ma Li' an expressed her point of view more than once: Without the social function played by urban village, Shenzhen will not achieve nowadays development speed and result and there would be no talent pool who support the city. Therefore, how to maintain the last "camp" for this group is what she wants to explore.

Ma Li'an is worried about current urban renewal programs, after which, only shopping malls and luxurious residential areas are built. And some urban villages are renewed by designers, only to be more expensive though prettier. If even the urban villages become expensive, where should the underprivileged and young people move to? The vast majority of these people then have to live beyond the Special Economic Zone fringe, which is even harder for them to integrate into the city. In fact, the existence of urban villages made it possible for them to live a colourful lifestyle in the city. In 2013, Ma Li'an initiated the "Urban Village Service Agent" public welfare organization to advocate community arts in all urban villages in Shenzhen in the hope of getting more people to know the surrounding environment through mutual exchange. In early 2014, Baishizhou was listed as the largest urban village to be renovated in Shenzhen. Ma Li'an, as project designer, organized a "Lab Rat" style project named "Handshake 302" to engage artists and crowds of curiosity from different countries to experience and explore the lives in the largest urban village in Shenzhen. Through artist expression, people gathered to discuss the phenomenon of the urban village, exchange ideas about its existence and make use of the platform to interact with people living in the urban village. They rented a room in a handshake building and designed interesting activities from time to time. For instance, she had designed an activity named "Counting". She nailed a row of shelves on the wall and asked participants to put on figures of salary and consumption with several light tubes on two sides. In the middle are the savings left over of every month. Through this form, she wants to remind people the reason why young people choose urban village. Through this "Lab Rat" style project, Ma and her team hope to get people who are out of the village to visit and reside in Baishizhou so that they can obtain varied inspirations and have different perceptions towards urban village and the renovation of these urban villages.

Ma Li'an's love for urban village is largely due to the harmonious relationship within the neighborhood. The children in Baishizhou is an active lubricant smoothing the community relationships. Most children in the urban village study at primary schools in the vicinity. They usually get off school before their parents get off work. Therefore, they would chase each other in the street and stare into the eyes of strangers with curiosity. Sometimes, they even came forward and ask all sorts of questions. Gradually, these kids are able to communicate with strangers boldly. Upon the influence of these kids, adults also slowly begin to get acquainted with each other. Every Saturday, when the "Handshake 302" activity was held, the neighbours next door would offer to help. In cold winter days, the hostess often came to visit her with hot Chaozhou "dim sum" or congee. The hostess's lovely children would greet her in English and Chinese. "This kind of harmonious neighborhood relationship is rarely observed in the highly developed community while on the contrary, courteous and polite children are more commonly seen in the urban villages. And you would not perceive it in the Overseas Chinese Town hundreds of meters away." In Ma Li'an's view, these are the positive energy and vigour in urban village.

Having been in Shenzhen for 22 years, Ma Li'an is often asked by others "Why do you stay in China for so long time?""Americans will not ask this kind of question, but the Chinese people will." She felt that it was a very interesting discrepancy. Ma Li'an's husband Yang Qian, is the founder of Fatbird Troupe, which Ma deems to be the most absorbing and entertaining theatrical troupe. "My husband is one of the reasons why I stay in Shenzhen, and the other one is that because China is so important and Shenzhen has changed the world so much." said Ma Li'an.

Couper:
Made a Great Fortune
as a Broker in Guangzhou

In 1845, the British merchant Couper set up Couper Dock in Changzhou Island, Huangpu District, Guangzhou, which is the first large scale industrial enterprise established by foreign capital in Guangzhou and also the first enterprise invested by foreign capital in China. Couper Dock was located in the northern part of Changzhou Island (current Huangpu Shipyard). The dock was named after John Couper himself. In 1845, the British Shipping Company employee John Couper from Scotland was sent by the company to Guangzhou and appointed the company's representative in Huangpu, responsible for supervision of the company's vessels' repairing work. After he arrived in Huangpu, he rented a few mud docks from the local Chinese people and hired a group of Chinese workers to engage in the ship repairing work. He, thus, soon became a capitalist from a supervisor. In order to expand the operation, he turned the mud dock into a stone dock, which people named "Couper Dock" after him. This was the first dock set up by foreigner in China, which embodied the beginning of China's modern shipbuilding industry.

In 1978, as Guangzhou took lead in the price "breakthrough", the model of "processing and compensation trades" (processing with supplied materials or given samples, assembling supplied components) commenced for the first time. In 1979, Mainland China's first export processing zone was established in Shekou. China 's economy reintegrated into the stream of the world economy. In the mid-1990s, the China Import and Export Fair which is referred to as "Canton Fair", attracted a large number of foreigners to engage in business activities in China. Arabs arrived first, followed by the Africans. They soon found that compared with Hong Kong, Guangzhou is more suitable for living and business. As a result of the chain effect, more and more Africans came here to catch up with the "gold rush". "East or west, digging gold in Guangdong is the best" was prevalent in China in the 1980s. Until today, the expression still applies to many foreigners. In the eyes of foreigners, the most profound impression Guangzhou left on them is not "the food in Guangzhou", but doing business in Guangzhou. In 2014, the Guangzhou Academy of Social Sciences released a survey "2014 Guangzhou City Internationalization Development Report", of which there is a part on Guangzhou city's international image. The survey showed that 58.6% of the respondents were impressed most by Guangzhou's "commerce", saying that commerce is highly developed in Guangzhou and there are a lot of potential opportunities while only 35.9% preferred the "Special Cuisine and Dim Sum".

In recent years, the businessmen in Huimei shopping mall and Kairongdu shopping mall have experienced the pressure from not only domestic counterparts, but also foreign businessmen, who try to take a share in the market. Mr. Zhang from the Northeast of China has encountered such competition several times. "Foreign customers came to our store to buy things and the sales girl at my shop began to talk to them in English. At this time, other foreigners came in and chatted with them. Then the foreign customers followed them and left. To start with, the sales girl thought they were acquaintances. Then we discovered it's not the case. Everytime foreign customers come in, those foreign competitors would come deliberately to persuade our customers to see products at their shops upstairs."

The shops on the eighth floor to the eleventh floor of Huimei shopping mall are all owned by foreigners. In the elevators, there are posters with clothing ads in English. In the past, these foreigners are Chinese businessmen's "guests", playing the role as purchasing agents. Since 2008, some foreign businessmen began to gradually penetrate into all aspects of foreign trade, bypassing the Chinese wholesalers and co-operate directly with the factories. "Through attending the Canton Fair, they got to know a lot of Chinese garment companies and were acquainted with each other gradually. These days they take goods from the factories and then do retail business or wholesale directly in the Zhanxi business district." said Mr. Zhang. It took only two to three years for those foreign businessmen to convert from being a purchasing agent to opening Taobao shops and from partnering with the "factory" to gradually running retail businesses and finally settled down with steady growing business in the Zhanxi business district. Sean from South Africa described Guangzhou as " a resourceful gold mine " . After running a bilateral wedding dress business between

China and Africa in Guangzhou for four years, he has made enough fortune and owned his own villa and a car in Cape Town. "The most expensive wedding dress purchased in Guangzhou was at the price of 1,200 yuan. Back to Cape Town, that wedding dress was sold out quickly at the price equivalent to at least 5,000 yuan." And their business is not limited to wedding dress, but also involves shoes, clothes, purses. In their views, Cantonese are very lucky as there are so many wholesale markets for them to explore and make a fortune.

In the area of "Xiaobei - Dengfeng - Huanshi Zhong Road", the congregation of Africans has come into existence for 10 years, and got the nickname of "chocolate city". And neighbours living in Dengfeng subdistrict joked: "I have got used to the smell of foreigner's perfume." Dengfeng subdistrict is well-known overseas, especially in the heart of Africans. The first photo of Albert taken in Guangzhou was at the entrance of Yueyang Business and Trade Plaza in Dengfeng subdistrict, neither the landmark Guangzhou Tower, nor Beijing Road, the ancient street with a thousand years' history. Dengfeng subdistrict, in their views, is the symbol of Guangzhou, which is good enough to tell "He has been to Guangzhou."

Aaron from Mali has been doing business in China for fourteen years and is able to speak Chinese fluently. When he was young, Aaron was also doing small business in Mali and imported commodities mainly from Southeast Asia. In 2002, Aaron, who held the idea "he would go there if fortune is there for him to make", followed his friends to Guangzhou as there were cheap suppliers in newly opened wholesale markets. He was overjoyed to strive for his own bright future before long he arrived in Guangzhou. "When I first came to Guangzhou, there were less African importers than today. Although I couldn' t speak Chinese, it' s quite smooth to do business with Chinese suppliers."Aaron said. Aaron started his business first in Guangzhou and slowly he expanded the supply chain to Qingdao, Fuzhou, Foshan, Dongguan Generally, he would choose some favourite clothing styles, and then put in orders in different factories. When Chinese New Year approaches, he goes back to Mali and sells them. It's just the flush time has passed. Africa's economy is going down. The business in Mali is even harder. The inventory imported from China risks overstocking. Nevertheless, Aaron does not intend to leave. "Compared to our country, chances are omnipresent in China. And I believe the African economy will recover slowly. I have been accustomed to working and living here." said Aaron.

Rafael Genis: International Startup Took Root in Shenzhen

The day was September 15, 2013. For the first time, young Israeli man Rafael Genis came to Shenzhen. "Wow, it is amazing. A lot of trees. Green scenery is everywhere!" On the way to Shenzhen city center, looking at the exuberant view outside the window, he could not hide his joy from the driver sitting next to him. Vigorousness is the first impression that this young city left on Rafael Genis: innovation, potential, bright future. Prior to this, he had been staying in Shanghai for three years. Then he was found by a headhunter to a white wine company in Shenzhen as brand development and marketing director. If you input "Israeli Rafael Genis" in Baidu.com, you will find a series of articles written by him: *Jews' Nine Tips to Get Successful, Is there Another Path Except for Success? Israeli Rafa Explores Unique Startup Culture, Israeli Entrepreneur*

Rafa Introduced Father in "Jewish Education" etc., which won him the reputation of "Israeli chicken soup prince" by his Chinese friends. To

▲ The day was September 15, 2013. For the first time, young Israeli man Rafael Genis came to Shenzhen." Wow, it is amazing. A lot of trees. Green scenery is everywhere!"

him, coming to Shenzhen has been the best decision of his life.

He had no concept of this city and did not expect too much before coming to Shenzhen. He stayed in Shanghai for three years, sort of tired and decided to leave out of pure curiosity and interest in new challenges. He knew nothing about Shenzhen except that it is a seaside city close to Hong Kong and there are many factories and enterprises. But having started business in Shenzhen for more than three years, he deemed Shenzhen as a big surprise. He often says to his friends that Shenzhen is by no other means, the future city of China. In addition, his love, trust and appreciation for Shenzhen lie in the fact that this city is quite similar to his homeland Israel-"entrepreneurial kingdom". In Shenzhen, Rafael has never felt that he is a "foreigner". His career goes smoothly and over the past half year, he was invited to give speeches at schools or enterprises for over 20 times where over 4,000 of his business cards were handed out. Like Israel, Shenzhen is a hub for immigrants. Wherever you go, no matter office or coffee shop or bar, it is very unlikely to meet local natives. These immigrants have become the engines of innovation as innovation is like connecting two different points and then creates a totally new point. The future of Shenzhen is like today's Israel, where almost all the parents of the children come from two completely different places. And each city in China has its own unique culture and customs so that they will bring different ideas and views. Nowadays, Rafael not only often posts articles about innovation and startup in the WeChat "moment" but also founded his own consulting firm, which provides service for those Chinese who

▲ Guangdong has become a paradise for foreign geeks.

want to visit and invest in Israel as well as the Israelis who wish to seek cooperation opportunities in China. Having been living in China for more than 6 years, he is fluent in Chinese and is knowledgeable about Chinese culture. "Shenzhen has experienced 38 years of development and change, where its population has risen from the original 300,000 people to the current 15 million people and the ignorant fishermen have now become young men who master the latest technology. Before 1979, China was relatively conservative. Since the reform and opening up, China officially opened to the West and has been developing rapidly for 38 years. Tremendous changes are still taking place. China is transforming from cheap exports to future innovation with high value.'Made in China'will be transited to'Created in China'. Can this vision be realised? Although it cannot be seen right now, by the strong support of the government and the enthusiasm of the Chinese people, I believe that the'Chinese dream'will eventually come true. " said Rafael.

For many geeks from the Silicon Valley in the USA, "Shenzhen" is not a strange word. Gathering in this area of almost 2,000 square kilometres are a lot of science and technology innovation park. Shenzhen as "China 's Silicon Valley" was repeatedly mentioned by foreign medias, which is the first thing they get to know about China. Someone compared the Silicon Valley to an engine, where you can smell the cutting-edge technology and future trends while Shenzhen is the place where such new technology can be applied to a variety of commercial areas rapidly and be brought into full play. Whenever there is a new creation in Silicon Valley, Shenzhen entrepreneurs are always the first to observe the change and they imitate and copy the new technology and create new opportunities. Tencent, the internet giant born in Shenzhen, is a standout among them. One of Tencent's most important products in the early period-OICQ was the imitation of one social software ICQ which enabled fast and direct communication on internet and was initiated by the Israeli youths Vigiser, Vardi and Goldfinger. In 1998, Tencent officially began the development of OICQ. Based on the imitation of ICQ, Tencent made another micro-innovation: Information was preserved from customers' end to the server side, which adapted to the internet environment in China at that time. Besides, Tencent invented the breakpoint transmission, group chat, screenshots and other functions successively. The development of Tencent's many products also reflected this feature. Someone concluded, "Tencent's 15 years of development is a history of business battle which relied on micro - innovation to defeat, one after another, rivals."

In 2015, Canadian "maker" Jessers arrived in Shenzhen and became a member of the international startups. The project he participated in is called "hardware accelerator" of HAX, whose headquarter was in San Francisco while the "accelerator" in China was in Huaqiang North Commercial Area, which mainly incubates hardware enterprises. French Homeric have been in Shenzhen for many years. He used to be an executive of a big headhunter company. He missed his family very much but the existing chat software failed to meet his needs. So, in December 2014, he resigned and started his own business with two friends to design an app named Shosha. This software would remind the "owner" to take a video of around 5 seconds every day. In Homeric's view, this casual "record" but not the staged photography nor flaunt shows the real life of the owner and is exactly what one's family hope to see. Speaking of Shenzhen Huaqiang North, Jessers exclaimed, "amazing." "Go downstairs and you can buy various components necessary for hardware innovation and design, whose prices are less than 1/3 of that in North America. Sometimes, you didn't bother to go outside and the sellers would show up with the components you needed." In fact, almost all "makers" who just arrived in Shenzhen are impressed by the convenience provided in Shenzhen. It is convenient to purchase all the hardware and also quite easy to find sales channels.

Christophe from France felt the same, "Hardware procurement process in the United States or Europe generally takes several days or even weeks, which is not a small cost for a start-up company."

Dongguan, 70 kilometres away from Shenzhen, is the famous "world factory". In September 1978, a Hong Kong-funded enterprise- Taiping Handbag Factory was established in Dongguan, becoming the first enterprise that processes raw materials on clients' demands, assembles parts for the clients and processes according to clients' samples and engages in compensation trade, which marked the advent of the industrialization of rural areas in Dongguan. China's economy has been inextricably connected to the world economy since then. With the development of processing trade in Dongguan, people once used the phrase "Dongguan stuck in traffic jam, the world out of stock" to describe the important position of Dongguan's manufacturing. In recent years, due to some deep- seated problems accumulated during the rapid development coupled with the impact of the international financial crisis, and as China's economic development marched into "New Norm", Dongguan suffered a bottleneck and faced a "double squeeze". In a new round of industrial transformation and upgrading, Dongguan has transformed from the "world factory" to "fertile soil for start-ups", especially high-tech enterprises sprung up like mushrooms after rain. Among them, there is an environmental technology company founded by the Italian Agostino. Agostino's company specializes in softened water, pure water and sewage' s treatment technology development and application. As environmental protection is increasingly valued, so is its sales, exceeding 100 million yuan nowadays. Agostino's experience in Dongguan is the epitome of the city's development. In 2006, Agostino accompanied his parents to come to Dongguan and attended a furniture factory. This was the first time for him to come to Dongguan. However, in 2008, manufacturing industry in Dongguan, which relied heavily on foreign trade exports, suffered a recession influenced by the international financial crisis. 857 foreign-funded companies were shut down or relocated. Agostino's parents also sold the furniture factory and returned home. However, Agostino was not willing to leave Dongguan, where his beloved girl, He Jiangyan from Shaanxi province, who is as beautiful as princess lives. Agostino remained and decided to find another path to operate a science and technology environmental protection company.

"Vacating cage to change bird", thus upgrading the industrial structure is one of the implemented measures by Dongguan government to cope with the crisis. An official of Dongguan said, since the reform and opening up, Dongguan has adhered to take export-oriented economy as the focus and thus lay the foundation for "World Processing Factory". But most of these enterprises in Dongguan are OEM producers or OEM branding producers, not much self-brand owners, while high added-value and huge profits were taken away by the branding merchants, the rest was the meagre manpower margins for the factories. "Vacating cage to change bird" namely transfer the existing traditional manufacturing industry out from the current industry cluster and then introduce the "advanced productive forces" in to achieve the purpose of economic transition and industrial upgrade. Agostino's decision coincided with the policy perfectly. Agostino and his wife joined together-Agostino takes care of the procurement and technology while He Jiangyan is mainly responsible for sales with government and enterprises. In addition to research and development as well as sales of environmentally friendly equipments, Agostino did not completely give up his old career. His company also deals with furniture sculpture equipment and vacuum packaging equipment. In 2006, Agostino introduced the top international professional wood engraving machinery from Italy, which can be used in the field of sculpture and ornament production. In 2008, again from Italy, he introduced the ORVED vacuum packaging machine and bags. He then has become the general distributor of the brand in Asia. Agostino has always felt lucky to make the decision to remain in Dongguan. Now he is financially free and lives a happy life with his wife and daughter. Over the past ten years, he has been accustomed to taking a walk or drinking tea with his wife and daughter every morning at weekends, looking at the crowd taking morning exercise and feeling the tranquillity and peace hidden behind the vigorousness and exuberance of the city.

百年
魚丸

小小魚丸五代傳

一九八〇年代一個冬日的凌晨，四時不到，天還未亮，梁志波撐開黏在一起的眼皮，踱至停泊在碼頭的漁船上驗魚鮮，天真冷啊。可秋冬季節的那哥魚也最肥美、鮮香，肉質潔白鮮美，正是做魚丸的上等材料。那時候，沒有冰塊也沒有冷藏技術，漁船一靠岸，這些做魚丸的工匠們就要立即將魚買下來開始打魚丸。梁志波捲起袖子，「那就開始吧」。做魚丸的第一道難關，是要使以多骨出名的那哥魚骨肉分離。梁志波憑藉多年的經驗，揚刀斬頭去尾、切肚起皮、剔骨挑肉，手起刀落之下，一條魚已經被處理乾淨。接著將魚鮮剁醬，置於特製的木桶中加調料，純用剛猛力快速捶打，這是做魚丸的第二道難關，不僅要恰當拿捏力度，還要憑藉經驗掌握時間。通常要捶打數千下，拍得不夠，膠漿不吐，魚丸鬆散而沒有彈性，拍打過度，魚漿變老，魚丸就沒有了脆和嫩的質感。這一步完了之後，梁志波抓起黏膠狀的魚漿握在手心，用力把魚漿從食指與拇指箍成的小圓圈中擠出來，放入冷水中，凝結了之後就該下鍋煮了。煮魚丸時，一絲絲的鮮香鑽入鼻孔，整個空間充滿魚的鮮甜，煮好的魚丸似重新被賦予了生命，在笠斗中上下彈動，散發著鮮香的熱氣。

二〇一六年十二月的一個早晨，梁志波的兒子梁少忠洗漱完畢，開車去到了食品廠，他準備視察、監督工人們的工作情況，順便給大家打打氣。二十分鐘的車程後，梁少忠到達了工廠，抬頭望門口的三行大字「繼承百年老字號，發揚傳統產業，開拓世界市場」。食品廠裡，梁少忠經過全身消毒後，進入了離門口最近的粗加工區，四個工人正在將剔好骨的魚放進絞肉機裡，不過幾秒鐘的時間，絞肉機就將碎狀的魚肉擠出，那邊精加工區的工人們也各司其職。因將生產魚丸的過程精細化，程式化，所以效率與三十年前相比，大大提升。一個工人推著手推車從身旁經過，三大箱剛出鍋的魚丸也隨車的顛簸而跳動，渾圓光潔，富有彈性而嫩、脆、香、鮮。兩個不同的時空彷彿突然因為相同的魚丸交錯了，一樣的配方，一樣的匠人技藝，一樣咬一口就讓人無限遐想的口味，就這樣從父親梁志波的手上傳承到了兒子梁少忠手裡。

汕頭，廣東省轄市經濟特區，東南沿海重要港口城市，粵東中心城市。說起汕頭，就不得不提潮汕商人。潮汕商人是中國傳統三大商幫之一。其淵源可追溯至明代，而與晉商、徽商相比，潮商歷久不衰，在世界範圍內影響深廣。有潮水的地方就有潮汕人，有錢賺的地方就有潮商。經過五百多年的商業洗禮，潮商已經成為中國實力雄厚、影響深遠、唯一沒有斷代的大商幫，是華人世界中富有的族群。他們信奉「有出息的男人不會待在家裡」，他們天生為了經商而存在，他們的血液裡流淌著商業細胞，他們拚搏進取、永不言敗，上演了一幕幕掘金大戲，發動了一場場經典商戰。新財富雜誌推出的二〇一六年「新財富富人榜」五百強中，來自潮汕地區富豪達三十六人，財富總和達 6895.9 億元。汕頭境內韓江、榕江、練江三江入海，大陸海岸線長 217.7 公里，海島岸線長 167.37 公里，有大小島嶼八十二個，其中的達濠島是一個著名漁港，水產品豐富，因魚丸而出名，這裡不大，卻有大小十幾家魚丸店。榮獲「中華名小吃」稱號的「晶華魚丸」更是其中的佼佼者。如今晶華魚丸在保持遵古法的基礎上，創新系列產品，如蝦丸，魚麵，墨斗丸等。著名美食家汪曾祺在品嚐晶華魚丸後說過這樣一句話：「沒吃過晶華魚丸，不算認識達濠。」

梁志波先生是汕頭市濠江區百年老字號「晶華魚丸」第四代掌門人。他嫻熟的製丸技藝，盡得祖輩真傳。大學畢業剛剛三年，作為第五代傳人的梁少忠，也接過了父輩的衣缽，在摸索中學習如何製作魚丸，如何管理企業，讓家族事業更好地傳承下去。

「晶華魚丸」創立至今已近一百三十多個年頭，由開山宗師梁晶合創立。在一百多年前，它只是一家小吃店，店裡的招牌菜是三大丸——魚丸、蝦丸、墨斗丸。二〇〇三年的一個契機，讓梁志波有了將晶華小吃店壯大的念頭。那年，潮汕籍的華僑回家鄉，品嚐到了美味的魚丸，他們將產品帶去了美國。家鄉的魚丸同樣俘獲了海外華僑的心，讓他們想起了家鄉的味道。慢慢地，有人找梁志波合作，想要他們生產魚丸送去美國，於是為適應市場需求，梁志波創辦了「汕頭市晶華魚糜食品廠有限公司」。目前，國內已有十三家晶華魚丸的連鎖店鋪，每天早上店裡的人都要趕到食品廠進貨，保證魚丸的新鮮。而在美國、香港等地，晶華魚丸也成功進入超市的貨架銷售。

不安分的接班人

　　梁志波有五個孩子，梁少忠排行老三。原本，大兒子才是梁志波最初定下要繼承家族產業的人，所以梁少忠的大哥在大學時讀的是食品加工專業。但慢慢地，大哥發現自己真正的興趣在於金融，梁志波沒有阻攔他，像以往一樣鼓勵孩子去做自己喜歡的事。於是，傳承的重任便落在了梁少忠頭上。現在，除了梁少忠在學習有關家族產業的知識外，其他兄弟姐妹都在銀行或者政府部門工作。梁少忠覺得，自己和兄弟姐妹能在自己喜歡的領域工作並且占有一席之地，與父親給予的民主的成長環境和最好的教育資源是分不開的。

　　大學畢業後，梁少忠著手學習企業的管理。本身對經商的興趣加上對傳統手藝的好奇與熱愛，讓大學學習物流專業的他轉變了自己未來的方向。他不服輸，憑什麼說只有日本的工匠能將他們的傳統手工藝發揚光大？他不允許，憑什麼讓成本越來越低的其他產品充斥市場？他想要保持並且擴張「晶華魚丸」這個品牌，將這門古老的手工藝保護起來，更進一步，提升整個達濠地區魚丸的其他產品價值和文化價值，讓更多人被達濠魚丸所「折服」。二〇一五年十二月，梁少忠去日本參觀學習其先進的管理經驗和製作工藝；二〇一六年三月，梁少忠帶領的「晶華魚丸」受香港潮屬商會總會的邀請作為潮汕美食的代表去參加香港的潮州節；十月，香港政府邀請他們去參加美食節。在美食節上，特區政府行政長官梁振英親自品嚐了魚丸，並且大加讚賞，梁振英的妻子現場購買了幾袋魚丸。

同年，梁少忠將目光轉向電商領域，現在，晶華魚丸除了入駐淘寶企業店鋪外，還入駐了兩個大型的電商平台，並且銷量可觀。為了使網購的魚丸也能最大程度地保留「晶華」特有的鮮甜，他摸索出一套讓網購顧客也能吃到最新鮮的魚丸的辦法。首先要注重魚丸的包裝以及儲存，他從外地引進保溫時長夠久的新型包裝材料，在魚丸中間加入冰塊，其次選擇最快的快遞公司，保證送到顧客手中時還是最新鮮最好吃的魚丸。他這一舉措也造福了家鄉的魚丸店，現在，達濠地區的魚丸店都普遍使用了新型保溫的包裝材料。

梁少忠接手後也遇到了一些現實的困難。「晶華魚丸」的宗旨是生產正宗的達濠魚丸，而這一宗旨的核心就是要使用最新鮮的魚，所以他們堅持採集附近漁港捕撈的新鮮魚肉作為原材料。但在十幾年前開始，中國大部分地區使用冷凍魚肉作為原材料，這樣不僅成本降低了，也有助於儲存和運輸。但「晶華魚丸」沒有變，他們始終堅持，不是新鮮的魚就造不出正宗的達濠魚丸。

而海洋資源的不穩定性以及稀缺性對漁業的影響非常大。天氣不好或沒魚的季節時，漁民們不得不休息，魚丸的生產也要隨之停滯。也因為魚丸的供貨非常不穩定，晶華魚糜食品廠有限公司也錯過了許多難得的發展機遇。香港的百佳集團以及廣東的黃振龍涼茶集團都曾與「晶華魚丸」有過合作，但大海有時並不那麼友善，它沒讓他們的合作繼續下去。

但擺在梁少忠面前的最大問題不是這些。做魚丸時上千次的猛力捶打、收集魚鮮時必須趕在大清早采貨讓許多年輕人退卻，企業因此面臨著人力資源匱乏的問題。不僅如此，由於工藝是仿古的，所以要將魚丸做好靠的是經驗以及老一輩傳授下來的技巧。這也使得魚丸沒辦法像工業生產一般，按照數據和標準進行通用化的生產，這進一步導致了人才的匱乏。不過他認為，「晶華魚丸」作為一個百年老字號，歷經風雨洗禮，雖然目前正面臨著嚴峻的挑戰，但晶華人決不會掉以輕心，也做好了迎接挑戰的準備。

梁少忠對未來亦是充滿了期望和規劃。首先，他想將顧客只是單純地到店裡或者網上購買產品的模式進一步完善，形成消費—旅游—再消費的可持續發展模式，將本地的魚丸產業打造成跟旅遊掛鉤的一個產業。他認為，通過日後進一步的擴大宣傳，讓更多的人認識晶華魚丸這個品牌。也許無意中購買的達濠晶華魚丸讓顧客對達濠產生興趣，進而來到不僅有魚丸，還有更多名勝古蹟的達濠古城遊玩。人們在旅游過後還能將魚丸帶回家中品嚐，或是接下來持續地在電子商務平台購買產品，一舉多得。「濠江區現在提倡做旅游城市，作為百年老店的『晶華魚丸』，毋庸置疑地要貢獻一份力量。日後晶華魚丸的總店可能會恢復幾十年前前店後廠的模式，通過展示生產工藝來吸引遊客。」梁少忠說。作為老一代的企業家，梁志波一直秉承著「酒香不怕巷子深」的理念，但在梁少忠看來，這樣的經營原則，在這個時代是行不通的。所以這幾年，「晶華魚丸」打起了廣告，開通了微博，還採用了時下流行的「轉發抽獎」模式。

梁少忠也考慮好了傳承的問題，誰來當掌舵人不是最重要的部分，重要的是做「晶華魚丸」這門古老的手藝和「晶華魚糜食品廠有限公司」企業以及企業的精神一定要傳承下去。他不會對將來的孩子有過多的要求和規劃，要像父親教育自己和兄弟姐妹一樣，讓孩子在一個輕鬆的環境下成長，根據興趣選擇專業和職業。如果孩子也熱愛這門傳統手藝且也想將它發揚光大，皆大歡喜，「晶華魚丸」將會成功擁有第六代傳人。如果孩子對這行不感興趣，梁少忠會考慮將公司打造成股份有限公司，任命職業經理人，繼續讓企業流傳下去，人們也能繼續吃到正宗的「晶華魚丸」。

吳浩和他的
浩天書店

從書癮少年到書籍「倒爺」

廣州文明路一四八號文德六巷，有一方約五十平方米的小天地。這個名為「浩天」的舊書店，宛如時光盒子，收藏了上世紀的時光。這個時代的風起雲湧，日新月異，彷彿都與它無關。在數字化洪流的侵襲下，傳統紙質書的發行，面對kindle、手機閱讀，就像一個躑躅前行的老人，舉步維艱。實體書店的經營，總是帶著點悲壯的氣質。在一片悲鳴聲中，從白雲區江夏到文明路，浩天書店走過了二十三個年頭。店主吳浩，靜靜地坐在一張籐椅上，日復一日、年復一年，守著三萬冊舊書古籍。

一九五九年，吳浩出生在文德路的一間平房裡。文德路位於廣州市越秀區，自古是書香興盛之地。作為文化街，與北京琉璃廠、上海城隍廟和南京夫子廟齊名，沿路歷來是古玩文物、古籍字畫、陶瓷、字畫裝裱等商店集中地，擁有相當悠久的歷史。在科舉制度盛行的清代，文德路以東修建廣州貢院，時有號舍五千間，為兩廣地區舉行鄉試場所，由此帶旺文德路一帶裱字畫，賣古董、書籍和文房四寶的店鋪。遇上科舉考試之年，數千考生流連於街市，或選購珍品，或欣賞古玩，一片繁榮景象。民國時期，此處設有六所中學，十家書店和廣東歐美同學會等十多個文化團體。新中國成立後，全省檔次最高、名家薈萃的文化團體——省戲劇家協會、省舞蹈家協會、省音樂家協會、省美術協會均匯聚於此。二十世紀八〇年代以來，這裡始終是嶺南屈指可數的老字號文化專業街。

吳浩在這條飄著油墨書香、聚集著文人雅士的街道里長大，對書籍有著特殊的情結。還在文德北三小讀書的時候，學校旁邊的廣州市兒童圖書館便是他的樂園。每當放學，小男孩便鑽進閱覽室裡，捧著一本又一本的連環畫，如飢似渴地閱讀著。有一回，吳浩看中了一本連環畫，每天去圖書館翻，愛不釋手。當時一本書一毛五左右，一頓早餐六分錢。他為了得到這本連環畫，連續餓了三個早上，終於在青年文化宮旁邊的兒童書店買到了，帶回家，每天照著臨摹，那種沉迷的勁頭，與如今的網癮少年，也並無二致。「書癮」少年嘗到了甜頭，每天挖空心思，琢磨如何找錢換書的法子，最後竟然想到了去撿橘子皮。在中醫裡，曬乾的橘子皮被稱為陳皮，廣東人素有用陳皮煲湯、入藥的傳統，可以理氣健脾，燥濕化痰。每個週末，吳浩都會去大街上、垃圾桶裡翻揀橘子皮，歡天喜地提著一小袋去收購站換錢。撿上一個月，換到的錢就夠買一本小人書了。在當時那個物資匱乏的年代，中國的老百姓最大的願望就是吃飽穿暖，吳浩的父母都是文盲，讓他們掏出錢來給孩子買書，那就是天方夜譚。從小到大，吳浩買的書，都是自己幾分錢幾分錢攢下來的，他的生意頭腦，也由此而來。只是，當時的書，總讓吳浩感覺有些「吃不飽」。在那個特殊的年代，書裡講到四大發明，只說是「勞動人民」發明的。可這些「勞動人民」都是誰呢？書裡沒有提。在谷歌、百度誕生的三四十年前，要想知道這些，只能去淘舊史書。於是，告別了挖空心思賺錢買連環畫的童年，少年吳浩燃起了對舊書的興趣。

一九五五年八月九日，北京青年楊華、李秉衡等人向共青團北京市委提出到邊疆區墾荒，並在十一月獲得北京市團委的批准與鼓勵，隨後引起城市知識青年到農村和邊疆墾荒的熱潮，毛澤東發出

「農村是一個廣闊的天地，到那裡是可以大有作為的」，「知識青年到農村去，接受貧下中農的再教育，很有必要」的指示。中國政府組織大量城市「知識青年」離開城市，發起在農村定居和勞動的群眾路線運動。一九七七年，高中畢業的吳浩下鄉到從化市（現在已是廣州從化區）鰲頭鎮。一九七八年十月，中國政府決定停止上山下鄉運動並妥善安置知青的回城和就業問題。一九七九年後，絕大部分知青陸續返回了城市，吳浩也回到了廣州，但戶口卻留在了農村。沒有戶口，就沒有工作，為了養家，頗有生意頭腦的他想出了自行印書去賣的「生財之道」。他先在北京路的舊書門市部買了一本教授如何油印的工具書。所謂油印，就是將蠟紙覆於鋼板上，用鐵筆在上面刻字，然後再滾上油墨印刷。吳浩那時候最愛聽的就是香港電台。在當時的政治環境下，這種行為還是不被允許的。於是他每天只能半夜十二點後，再扭開收音機，趴在桌前，一邊聽一邊記錄，直到凌晨兩三點。然後自行刻字、印刷、裝訂，用這一簡便技術，把從香港電台裡聽來的內容印刷成兩百本名人格言和談吐藝術，帶到北京路新華書店門口售賣。這些書在當時可算是希罕物，僅有的兩百本書洛陽紙貴，印刷成本五分錢，賣出去五角錢，幾天工夫就賣完了，讓吳浩著實賺了一筆。可在他收拾攤子準備離開時，兩個街道辦的工作人員以他的行為屬於「投機倒把」為由，將他送去了派出所。所幸民警只是把他教育了一通，讓他反省了一晚上，便擺擺手讓他回去了，連賺來的錢都沒有沒收。吳浩歡天喜地回到家裡，只是以後再也不敢自行印書售賣了。嘗到了甜頭的他，明白在那個年代，人們對知識、對書籍的渴求，因此便換了一種方式，依舊以賣書為生。在他被教育了不久後，新華書店開始售賣之前十多年裡被封存的書，有唐詩宋詞、世界名著等。知識青年們對這些書籍的追捧，與今日瘋狂追星的年輕人並無二致，新華書店每天都要上演被瘋狂搶書的「盛況」。由於「人多書少」，新華書店限量售賣，每人每天限買兩套，還不能選擇，只能隨機購買。這當然無法滿足如飢似渴的知識青年們。吳浩從中嗅到了商機，閒來無事的他，每天凌晨兩三點就在書店門口排隊，到新華書店早上九點開門時，門前已經聚起了長長的人龍。吳浩常常能排在隊首，每天能買到兩套書，一套書有二到四本。吳浩買到書後，拿到市場上倒賣。五到六元買回來的一套書，在市場上能賣到十三四元。十幾天下來，他又賺了一百多元。新華書店的封存舊書賣完後，吳浩只得另想賺錢的法子。不久後，他成為了天光墟的一名「掮客」，用他的話說，是七十二行之外的奇怪行當。天光墟是廣州民間集市，每天清晨或半夜開始營業，天亮即歇業的特殊墟，故得此名（粵語「天光」即「天亮」），因此「天光墟」一名只在粵語地區出現。以擺賣舊家具、器皿、故衣、什架等二手廉價貨物及古董、字畫、古籍、盆栽等為主，清末民初為其全盛時期。如今，廣州尚存的「天光墟」命運各不同。海珠中路舊書天光墟每週六開，至今仍在經營。濱江路「跳蚤市場」每天清晨營業到中午。芳村大道西「花墟」每天凌晨營業到上午。文昌路文物「天光墟」每週二清晨「開墟」。華林玉器天光墟正在改造升級。荔灣路舊電子產品、舊貨天光墟則已經消失。二十歲的吳浩游走於海珠中路和文昌路的「天光墟」，靠著「倒買倒賣」，收入並不比他那些有穩定工作的朋友們差。

尋路「十年計畫」

一九八〇年，吳浩的戶口遷回了廣州。在大多數人的心目中，有一份穩定的工作方是正途，也有社會地位。於是，有了戶口的吳浩，進入了廣州市第八機械廠，成為了一名機械一級工，月收入有三十多元。當時的中國，已經邁出了改革開放的步伐。一九八〇年十二月十一日，十九歲的浙江溫州姑娘章華妹從溫州市工商行政管理局領到了一份特殊的營業執照。這張用毛筆填寫的並附有相片的營業執照，成了中國第一份個體工商戶營業執照，她本人則成為中國第一位個體工商戶。而在廣州，出生於書香人家的容志仁，在家附近開了一家「榮光」飲食店。在上世紀八〇年代初，「容光」飲食店每天都可以賺到一兩百元，多的時候一天可以賣出三百斤豬腸粉。一九八一年，作為個體戶代表之一，容志仁被時任省委書記任仲夷接見，擔任了廣州個體勞動者協會會長。之後，他又先後受到鄧小平、胡耀邦的接見，一時傳為創業佳話。而在廣州高第街，更是走出了一個又一個的「萬元戶」。一向心思活絡的吳浩呆不住了，一九八七年，他扔掉鐵飯碗，「下海」成為了一名「個體戶」。這是吳浩「做生意」數十年來唯一一段與舊書、古玩無關的經歷。當時的文德路已發展成為鏡框、相框一條街。做這些生意需要比較大的本錢，而且已經成行成市，再去分一杯羹，其實並不容易。吳浩的想法是「我競爭不過你們，那我就跟你們合做作生意」。於是，他搞起了運輸。文德路上的鏡框、相框，大部分都是賣到香港的。吳浩東拼西湊出一萬多元，買了一輛零點六排量的小貨車，和這些鏡框店的老闆們做起了生意。鏡框店有了訂單，他去工廠拉貨，直接送到港口，每天的營收都能達到一百多元，扣除成本，每天的利潤有五十多元，一個月淨賺一千五六百元，這在當時絕對算得上是高收入。運輸生意做了七年，積累了本錢，吳浩再一次轉行，做起了自己最熟悉的老本行──賣書。生於文德路、長於文德路，從小與圖書館為鄰的他，對書總有一種揮之不去的情結。文德路以前就是書店一條街，最鼎盛的時候，一條街上有三十多家書店。而他從小的夢想，就是開書店。吳浩走的是一條「城市包圍農村」的道路。上世紀八○年代，席絹、瓊瑤的言情小說，古龍、金庸等人的武俠小說已經風靡大陸。當時，娛樂方式還非常匱乏，人們閒暇時間，除了看電視之外，最喜歡的休閒方式，就是捧著小說，體味江湖中人的快意人生或是青年男女間的纏綿悱惻。而在廣州的城鄉結合部，書店還很少，年輕人到城裡買一本書並不容易，而且他們這些小說好讀，三五天就能看完一本，大部分人的經濟能力也不允許他們一本接一本地買。一九九四年，吳浩搬離了市中心的文德路，在白雲區黃石路，以前店後居的方式，經營了自己的第一家「浩天書店」，專門租售各類書籍。租書價格為一天五角錢，一時間，浩天書店門庭若市，一天的營業額就能達到三百元。

　　吳浩在黃石路一住七年，直到二○○三年，他將「浩天」搬回了與家中舊屋一街之隔的文明路。此時，圖書市場早已不復當年盛況，廣州不少曾經頗受追捧的書店，在短短幾年內，前赴後繼地默默關張。儘管哀嘆聲一片，國人閱讀的頻次越來越低卻是不爭的事實，「浩天」也難掩落寞景象，然而吳浩卻仍在信心百倍地施展他的「第二個十年計畫」。「我早就有了三個十年計畫了。第一個十年計畫已經實現了，就是賣書租書，現在已經實現了。第二個十年計畫，是做精品。現在的圖書市場，打的都是價格戰。我不隨波逐流，我做的就是精品書。第三個十年計畫，我要做微型博物館。因為我是有計畫的，所以現在我能定得住，不焦慮。」吳浩所做的精品，其實還是老本行，就是去天光墟「淘寶貝」。幾年經營下來，浩天成為了廣州數得上名號的舊書店。在這期間，他也確實做過幾筆很讓人滿意的買賣。他曾經在天光墟淘到了清代詩人張維屏所撰寫的一副對聯，以三百元的價格買入，最終以三千元價格賣出。他還自言，淘到了康熙十年的一本佛經，這是「浩天」的「鎮店之寶」，當時以五百元的價格買入。吳浩對於自己的眼力非常自信，自言不會買到贗品。之所以認定佛經確實是康熙年間的古籍，是因為當時的紙張與現在不同，更加透明，手感也更有韌勁，現代的紙張生產工藝，已經不會再生產這樣的紙張了。這本佛經，至今藏在吳浩家中，待價而沽。「這是寶貝，我不著急賣，也極少與人說起。」

長年與古書為伴，「修補舊書」也成了吳浩的絕活。他為一本本舊書重新釘上封面，或者套上透明的保護套，有的書紙張經過風乾已經發脆了，他用保護膜一張一張地套好。為了提高銷售量，吳浩和妻子羅姨也曾經嘗試過網絡化經營的方式，兩人花了五千元購置了一台電腦，在中國最大的古舊書網絡交易市場——孔子舊書網上開了一家網店，網頁維護技術卻成為了橫在兩人面前的「攔路虎」。因為不會操作，電腦一死機，夫妻倆就陷入了手足無措的境地。網店需要更新書目，還要網頁維護。若要請人幫忙設計網頁，就得花費幾百上千。大量瑣碎的事情花費了夫妻倆太多的精力，甚至影響了實體店的經營。半年後，「浩天」就結束了網店生涯。

　　吳浩的第三個十年計畫，是把「浩天」打造成微型博物館。如今，「浩天」確實在城中文藝青年群體中有了點名氣。店裡的布置，全是吳浩一手設計，除了各種古舊書籍，店鋪中央掛著一口停止的鐘，天花板上，吊著舊時裝零錢的籮筐、古舊的手風琴、秤桿和秤砣，櫥窗裡陳列著以前的電影票根、收藏錢幣，書櫃上放置著二十世紀五六十年代流行的搪瓷臉盆、綠色的軍用水壺。這些都是每周吳浩去天光墟淘來的「寶貝」。

　　幾個年輕人在店裡徘徊，與其說他們是買書的，不如說是來拍照的。將照片放到朋友圈裡，曬一曬情懷，是當下年輕人愛做的事。

　　對此，吳浩也是見怪不怪了。雄心壯志抵不過現實，「浩天」如今的狀況，也不過是基本上收支相抵，賺不了多少錢。「浩天」的名氣，能吸引到一些人，但總是看的人多，買的人少。小資青年來此，也不過是拍幾張照片，買幾張明信片。吳浩的妻子羅姨對於生活充滿了憂慮，每當看到來拍照，只逛不買的人，她便會煩躁。在她的堅持下，「浩天」立了「規矩」，不買東西就不得拍照，用羅姨的話來說，是「經營不易，要想來看新鮮，就得支持一下」。可吳浩對此總拉不下臉來，妻子不在店裡的時候，遇上年輕人來閒逛拍照，他只是靜靜地坐在籐椅上，聽之任之，不願意開口讓他們買東西。每每妻子回來看到此情形，就免不了生氣。在網上，也有關於「浩天」的一些微辭，例如接受採訪，收費是每小時一百元。這也是羅姨立下的「規矩」，但這其中並非不能變通：想聽「浩天」的故事，就要買東西支持一下。金額不限，採訪者自己看著給。如果什麼都不買，採訪收費每小時一百元。吳浩對羅姨很是尊重，只要是妻子在場，店裡的事情妻子說了算，只會對採訪者抱以歉意的微笑，說著：「不好意思，謝謝理解。」「他分了精力跟你們講故事，就顧不上店裡的生意了。我們店裡經常丟書，還有些小年輕，拿了明信片就走，被我叫住了，才說不知道是要給錢的。我們現在生存不易，手停口就停。」羅姨言語中，已頗有些抱怨之意。吳浩在一旁，默不作聲。年少的他，有著許多的雄心壯志，以書做生意，為謀生，為投資。如今的他，更多的是堅守與情懷。他與書相依相偎了二十餘載。如今「功未成」，卻已起了「身退」之意，准備把店鋪交給妻子打理。有人曾經用「文化沙漠中的烏托邦」來形容「浩天」，而守業者吳浩，面對互聯網的洶湧浪潮，又像與風車搏鬥的堂吉訶德。麵包與夢想能否共存？願下一個十年，廣州仍有「浩天」。

周沖：
我是托舉哥

打工仔

二〇一二年六月三日，為了救被陽台防盜網卡住的女童，周沖徒手從三樓的防盜窗逃生口爬出去，用一隻手托住女童，為營救工作爭取了必要的時間。一個六分鐘的托舉動作，改變了周沖的一生。他從一個還在為找工作發愁的年輕人，成為了名人，獲得讚譽無數。不僅找到了工作，還得以落戶廣州。在百度新聞裡輸入「周沖」，彈出的第一條是二〇一六年三月二十四日的新聞——「技術工人周沖當選廣東省青聯副主席」。除了敬佩、讚歎之外，許多人還會感嘆周沖「命好」。但其實他本可以更幸運，只是當各種月薪過萬的經理、主任的職位砸向他的時候，他選擇了做回老本行——成為廣州港集團的一名維修工。這並不意味著他胸無大志，他只是想做自己能勝任的，再依靠真本事，實現人生的向上流動。「我不想被人說閒話，我爸媽更不想，他們天天念叨我，我的耳朵都聽出老繭了。」四年了，周沖沒有後悔這個選擇。說起四年前轟動一時的「托舉」，他依然會謙遜地認為「這只是一件小事」，但是說起工作，他言語中有著掩蓋不了的自信。「我在這個崗位上幹了四年，沒有誰說過我不行的。」四年前，周沖用雙手托起了生命，在過去、現在以及將來，周沖還是用這雙手，托起了自己的一片天。

一九八九年，湖北孝感市孝昌縣周巷鎮的周玉明和宋秀英夫婦迎來了他們的第一個孩子。男孩長得虎頭虎腦，單眼皮的小眼睛滴溜滴溜，盡是靈氣。周玉明夫婦看著這個一臉聰明相的孩子，滿是欣喜，給他起名「周沖」，希望他有衝勁，日後闖出一片天。然而，由於生活所迫，周沖父親不得不長期外出打散工，以補貼家用。年幼的周沖，很少有機會看到爸爸，只能和媽媽相依為命。後來，弟弟妹妹相繼出生，家裡經濟狀況更是捉襟見肘。等三個孩子到了上學的年齡，每到交學費的時候，父親就愁得吧嗒吧嗒地抽菸。作為老大，周沖十三歲時就挑起家中的一些重活，插秧、割稻、拉板車，他全都在行。二〇〇五年，初中畢業，成績平平無望上重點高中的周沖南下廣州，投奔天河區的堂兄。後經人介紹，他在員村一家超市當了一名導購員。入職十九天後，便是發工資的日子，周沖拿到了兩百元。初到廣州的日子裡，周沖唯一的花銷，就是每個週末自掏飯錢，花兩元吃一份素炒河粉。其餘的日子裡，老闆包吃包住。周沖把兩百元存起來，準備過年回家交給父母。當時的他，對於金錢並沒有什麼概念，兩百元對於他來說，是一份希望的開始：十九天就能攢下兩百元，一年下來將近四千元，家裡多了這些錢，到時爸媽就不用那麼辛苦了。然而，在工作了三個多月後，他第一次和室友一起逛了逛廣州的商場，才發現世界根本不是自己想像的那個樣子。在天河城裡，買一件最普通的上衣，都得花掉一個月的工資。從此，他便很少外出了，一心撲在了工作上。然而，無論他多努力工作，依然能深深地感覺到自己是這座城市的邊緣人：掙得少，一無所長，高薪職業根本輪不上他，看不到任何發展的希望。周沖不願意這樣虛耗光陰，在底層苦苦掙扎。於是，他決定離開廣州，到貴州大伯那裡學電焊技術。二〇〇五年年末，在廣州度過了大半年的周沖，帶著超市老闆結算的工錢，黯然返鄉。十六歲少年的城市夢，還沒來得及開始，就結束了。

回老家住了幾天後，周沖便待不住了。他已經開了眼界，現狀讓他焦慮。急於改變的他等不到過年，便帶著三百多元路費前往貴州。大伯把他介紹到貴州遵義一個銲接師傅那裡：包吃包住當學徒，但沒有薪水。條件雖苛刻，可周沖還是答應了。在之後的一年裡，周沖每天凌晨四點起床，四點半開工，抬鐵箱子、切割鐵皮，要趕在早上八點鐘吃早餐；之後，接著幹到下午二點吃午飯，完後再加班加點，直至凌晨零點多收工。二〇〇六年到二〇〇七年，是周沖人生中最難熬的時候，每天坐著都能睡著。身體的極度疲累讓他連思考的力氣都沒有了。由於師傅當時是拉私活，他並沒學到多少實際的電焊技術。兩位師兄後來不時會讓周沖摸摸電焊機，他抓住機會實際操作了幾回。最窘迫的時候，他連洗髮水都買不起，頭皮癢得實在受不了了，抓一把洗衣粉往頭上搓。在這樣異常艱苦的情況下，周沖咬牙堅持了近兩年。二〇〇八年初，拿著五百元的工資，他再度踏上了回家之路。只是，與兩年前不同，此時的他，已經有了手藝，內心也篤定多了。不久後，他在武漢江漢區一家工地做電焊工，在四年多的時間裡，薪水從一千多元漲至五千多元。有了「核心競爭力」的他，又開始規劃起自己的人生——當一個包工頭，在城裡包下工程，從老家帶工人出來做。以後，甚至可以當老闆。這一年的他，二十三歲，世界豁然開朗。他有了無限的機會，無盡的可能。他以為自己終將在武漢闖出一片天，卻不知道，因緣際會之下，將與廣州再度結緣。

二〇一二年三月，周沖的父親周玉明給鄰村一戶李姓人家裝修房屋，因為缺人手，周沖也臨時回去幫忙。李家在廣州打工的女兒李英，也因為房屋修繕而回家幫忙。第一次見面，周沖便喜歡上了這個大眼睛的姑娘。李英也對陽光帥氣的周沖頗有好感。只是，武漢和廣州的距離讓她感到頗為猶豫。為了打消姑娘的顧慮，周衝決定辭去工作，重返廣州。工地老闆是真心喜歡這個踏實肯幹的小夥子，得知周沖為了追一個姑娘，寧願放棄這份待遇不錯的工作，便勸他：「現在五千多元一個月的工作也不是隨隨便便能找得到的，你到了廣州，誰知道會是個什麼境況。如果找不到工作，一無所有，姑娘能跟著你麼？」周沖對此義無反顧：「我想做的事情，是一定會去做的。」他的誠意和果敢打動了李英的芳心，兩人很快確定了男女朋友的關係。二〇一二年五月二十二日，周沖牽著女友，回到了他闊別七年的廣州。然而，儘管有技術在身，尋工的過程卻並沒有他所想像得那麼一帆風順。來到廣州後，一切都得重新開始，別人也不知道他的能力。找了好幾個地方，要麼說他太年輕了，經驗缺乏，要麼說不需要人了。無奈之下，周沖只能暫時幫在廣州的堂哥照看他的小賣部。每天從中午開始看鋪，到半夜一兩點，早上七八點就開始在外面找工作。

托舉哥

二○一二年六月三日上午，周沖和李英一起前往東圃找工作。女孩琪琪命懸四樓花架。正陪女友出門找工作的周沖在千鈞一髮之際，不顧個人安危，爬出窗外，托著琪琪的雙腳長達八分鐘，這一托，徹底改變了他的命運。《南方都市報》記者謝亮輝詳細記錄了當時驚險又激動人心的一幕：三歲女孩琪琪因為被反鎖在房間裡，為了尋找出門的辦法，她爬上了房間陽台的空調主機，再翻上比她還要高的陽台護牆，想從這個途徑爬進隔壁書房。然而在空置的鋁合金花架上，琪琪整個身子漏了下去，頭卻卡在了上面，整個人懸掛在空中。

十一時三十分，路人小范聽到了琪琪的哭聲，他抬頭一看，大聲驚呼：「有小孩要掉下來啦！」街坊們聞訊趕來，幾名男子小跑到琪琪下方，伸出雙手做出托舉的動作，生怕孩子就這樣掉了下來。有街坊則迅速跑到樓上，努力拍打琪琪家門，卻無人應答。

十一時三十一分，樓下店鋪老闆找來三個紙盒，擺放在地面上，希望能起到緩衝的作用。旁邊兩夫妻，拉著家裡正使用的黃色被單，一路小跑到事發地點。四名男子立即分四角拉開，隨時準備接住琪琪。樓下的潘姨得知消息後，也趕緊打開防盜窗的鎖，讓街坊出去施救。路過此地的周沖，此時也跟著熱心的街坊們跑進了潘姨的家中。

十一時三十二分，怡東苑小區清潔工周先生，和妻子先後搬出家裡的兩個床墊，鋪在被單下面的地上。

十一時三十五分，天河交警黃漢初趕到現場，他一邊查看現場情況，一邊用對講機請求支援。另一邊，因為潘姨家防盜窗所留的窗空隙口太小，幾名男子試圖爬到窗外將琪琪救下，但都因身子太大無法進入。這時候，琪琪已經沒有力氣了。原本握著花架的手都鬆開了，頭還卡在上面動彈不得，呈現出一種「上吊」的姿勢。

　　十一時三十六分，身穿黃衣的周沖出現在了監控鏡頭中。孩子在四樓，周沖從三樓的防盜窗往上爬，花架正好卡在琪琪的喉嚨處，孩子的眼淚已經哭乾了，嘴邊上開始出現了白沫。因為個頭不高，周沖踩在防盜窗最下面的時候，頂著孩子的腳卻用不上力，於是，他又往上爬了一格，讓琪琪的腳踩在自己手上，讓琪琪的頭不會再卡在花架上。孩子這時候已經緩過勁來了，又開始哭。周沖再往上爬到了防盜窗第三格的位置，保持左手扒著外牆，右手托舉的動作。此時，一名街坊拿出一把繩索跑來，系在周沖的腰間，另一人則透過窗戶抱住他的腳，避免發生意外。

　　十一時四十二分，天河交警大隊東圃中隊副中隊長丘仁賢從車陂的一單事故現場趕來。在他的指揮下，街坊們衝到琪琪家門外，強行破門救人。

　　十一時四十五分，花架被鋸斷。琪琪被嚇得魂飛魄散的外公抱在了懷中，周圍響起一片掌聲。此時的周沖，自己默默地爬下了防盜網，與李英和侄子一起，悄然離開了現場。

　　然而，周沖的身影已經留在了監控攝像頭和市民自發拍下的視頻中，他的救人義舉席捲了網絡，廣州發起了全城大搜索。各路媒體通過電視循環播放尋人啟事：「身高大約一米七八，身材魁梧，外地人，市民有任何關於這個男人的信息，可以跟天河區街道聯系，天河區希望能給予他相關獎勵。」新浪微博也發出「好人通緝令」：時間：六月三日上午十一時三十分。地點：天河區東圃怡東苑小區。事由：三歲琪琪脖子卡在四樓陽台花架上身體懸空，無名黃衣男青年冒著生命危險用一隻手托舉直到孩子獲救！事後一去不返毫無音訊！你知道他在哪？網友都來「通緝」他！與此同時，也有不少反對尋找的聲音。「既然他希望留在人們心中的只有行為，為什麼要挖掘他的身分呢？」「是誰沒關係，只要提倡這精神，何必搞人肉搜索，這樣只會扭曲了助人者的心意，令某些人以為他作秀，博出位。」

六月九日，周沖被媒體找到，在接受了輪番採訪報導後，他的面孔被無數人記住。人們親切地稱他為「托舉哥」，還上了央視的《新聞聯播》。他成為了二〇一二年廣州城裡最著名的平民英雄。周沖被突如其來的一切砸得有些發懵，到廣東才十多天的他，並不知道大半年前，發生在佛山的「小悅悅事件」，是許多廣東人心中抹不去的痛。二〇一一年十月十三日，二歲女孩小悅悅在佛山南海黃岐廣佛五金城相繼被兩車碾壓，七分鐘內，十八名路人路過但都視而不見，漠然而去，最後，一名拾荒阿姨陳賢妹上前施以援手。現場監控視頻被發布在網上後，震驚世人。二〇一一年十月二十一日，小悅悅經醫院全力搶救無效，在零時三十二分離世。二〇一一年十月二十三日，廣東佛山二百八十名市民聚集在事發地點悼念小悅悅，宣誓「不做冷漠佛山人」。二〇一一年十月二十九日，設有追悼會和告別儀式，小悅悅遺體在廣州市殯儀館火化，骨灰將被帶回山東老家。人們太需要正能量了，周沖和他身後眾街坊的出現，猶如黑暗中的一道閃電，照亮了人心。

二〇一二年六月十三日，時任中共中央政治局委員、中央書記處書記、中宣部部長、中央文明委副主任劉云山接見了全國各地的楷模代表，周沖在接見之列。

▌電焊工

相比起榮譽獎金，更讓周沖感到欣喜的，是接踵而至的工作機會。短短兩天，廣州已先後有十一家國有企業向他發出了就業邀請。這其中有一些職位，是曾經想都不敢想的。「有一個很著名的地產公司讓我去當副經理，負責項目現場的運作和監督。還有一家單位願意提供辦公室副主任的職位，管理整個園區的環衛和安保工作，月薪上萬，有獨立辦公室，配一房一廳的宿舍，還有專車接送。」面對這些突如其來，又讓人豔羨無比的工作機會，周沖並非沒有動心過。然而，他最終選擇成為廣州港集團的一名電焊維修工。相比起其他工作機會，這是一份比較艱苦的工作，技術要求高，對身體可能會造成一定的傷害，薪酬待遇也談不上誘人，卻能求個心安理得。成名之後，媒體也蜂擁至他的家鄉採訪，父母高興之餘，也挺擔心的。選工作那段時間，周玉明每天給兒子打電話，囑咐他別接受與自己能力不相符的事情，讓別人說閒話。老實巴交的周玉明夫婦，一輩子最怕被人說閒話，同樣的話翻來覆去地說，周沖覺得耳朵都聽出了繭，然而他終究是聽進去了。除了考慮待遇問題，他更多的還是考慮自己的能力能否勝任。而廣州港的工作，可以說是為周衝量身定做的工種，周沖之前就有六年的電焊經驗，加上廣州港集團已經為他制定了一系列的培養計畫，在這裡，他可以憑藉自己的能力成長。如果貿然接受了一個經理的職位，肯定是不能服眾的。憑什麼人家爬了十幾年才能爬到的位置，托一個小女孩幾分鐘，就把本該屬於別人的位置占了呢？

在電焊工的位置上，周沖感到有底氣，也很自信，每一步都走得踏實。他利用業餘時間到廣州港技校參加中專學習，二〇一五年六月拿到了中專文憑。緊接著又報讀了機械一體化的大專課程，未來還要繼續升本科。他的人生規劃非常清晰：本科階段學一些管理方面的知識，爭取在三十五歲之前拿下碩士學位。二〇一四年，在廣州港集團舉行的市二類電焊維修比賽中，周沖一舉獲得第一名，升級為高級焊工。二〇一五年，他又因工作成績突出，被評為廣東省勞動模範。「我在這個崗位上工作了四年，沒有一個人說我不行，一般的維修我都能搞得定，可以獨當一面。」周沖的家安在距離港口約三四公里的單位宿舍，喧囂退去後，他的生活過得平靜而充實：

七時十五分騎自行車出門，七時三十分左右就能到單位，七時四十五分到七時五十分開工前會，中隊長佈置一天的工作後，大家開始各自幹活。如果當天沒有電焊維修工作，周沖就給機械做一些基礎保養，輔助中隊長整理材料以及其他的基礎管理工作。

十一時四十五分吃中午飯，如果有搶修，吃完飯就得開工，正常的情況下，下午十四時上班，直到十七時下班。成名後的這幾年裡，周衝去過很多大學做講座，年輕人最愛問的問題是：「你換女朋友了麼？」周沖有些哭笑不得。他和李英在二〇一三年四月結婚，如今已經有了一個兩歲的女兒。妻子是一名辦單員，兩個人一個月的薪水加起來不超過一萬，說不上太低，但若想在廣州買房，還是緊巴巴的。如今，周沖正在存錢買房。對於許多外來工而言，不在廣州買房，即使有了廣州戶口，也算不上真正的廣州人。周沖從不隱藏自己的「野心」，他並不滿足一輩子當一個電焊工，如今

不斷地進修，也是希望有朝一日，能走上管理崗位。「這個要想，
必須要想，怎麼能沒有目標，沒有夢想呢？」

▌公益人

　　二〇一六年三月，已經逐漸從公眾視野中淡出的周沖，名字再次出現於報端。三月二十三日，《廣州日報》報導，廣東省青聯十屆四次常委（擴大）會議在廣州召開。增選「托舉哥」、廣東省青年五四獎章獲得者、青年技術工人周沖為省青聯副主席。廣東省青聯的工作與公益分不開，自從在二〇一二年成為「托舉哥」後，周沖便與公益結下了不解之緣。最初，他對「公益」並沒有什麼概念。剛成為「托舉哥」那會兒，活動邀請特別多，都要經單位批准。不僅是在廣東的，還有在省外的，邀請函發到集團，領導審批同意，他就得去，上一個月的班，有半個月都不在崗位上，在外面做活動。最初，他會感到有些吃不消，面對同事也會生出幾分歉意。直到在二〇一三年九月的一次扶貧活動中，他的靈魂受到了觸動，真正明白自己從事的活動，對需要幫助的人來說，意味著什麼。那是一次去清遠一個貧困村的扶貧活動，一行人下了車，來到一個土磚院子門前。院子沒有大門，裡面是幾進小屋，每間小屋都是連一個像樣的門都沒有，只有兩根木頭，支起一個布簾。聽到了聲響，一個骨瘦如柴，駝著背的老大爺從屋子裡顫顫巍巍地走出來。志願者們把米、油、棉被送進屋子裡。老人家握住周沖的手，眼淚啪噠啪噠往下掉，落在周沖的手上。周沖也哭了，此後，每次談及自己的公益之路，他都會提起這件事情。

　　周沖從二〇一二年開始參加各類志願服務、公益慈善活動，至今，他利用工作之餘參加的公益活動不少於兩百場。黃埔區志願驛站以他的名字命名，天河區也有周沖的驛站，除了上班、學習、睡覺，周沖其餘的時間幾乎全花公益上。他還帶動家人一起做公益，妻子在工作之餘，就經常幫他派發公益宣傳單。光環能夠帶動社會，號召大家去幫助別人。但不管有沒有光環，我們每個人作為社會的一分子，都應該在各方面為社會做一些貢獻。周沖說，不管以後自己的名聲還在不在，依然希望能通過自己去感染身邊的人，通過自己的雙手去讓大家看到社會上的正能量。

向上流動

外來工也能讀北大

二〇一二年九月二十九日，廣州農民工博物館開館。作為中國首個農民工博物館，位於廣州白雲區馬務村的農博館，通過約五千件實物講述了農民工自己的故事。農民工博物館是由白雲區馬務聯和工業區十二號舊廠房「原汁原味」改建成的，並以這一博物館為核心，建設了廣州城市印記公園，再現改革開放以來農民工發展變化的歷程。四層展館分「總序」「孕育與發展」「走進億萬農民工」三個主題對農民工工作、歷史、生活等方方面面進行了全面的回顧。一樓的生產車間原貌展廳更是將整條製鞋、製衣流水線「搬」進了博物館。在「安全生產重於泰山」的橫幅下，眾多針車、機器、原材料、鞋衣半成品占據展廳，投影儀在牆壁上通過視頻再現農民工忙碌的工作場景。農博館二樓「孕育與發展」展廳，則按時間順序講述了近百年來農民工歷史。「農民工」這一稱謂的最早表述來自於這裡的一件展品──一九八四年第一期的《社會學通訊》。該展廳還模擬修建了一輛從成都至廣州的綠皮火車，火車四個窗口通過視頻還原了火車內場景。

三樓和四樓的「走進億萬農民工」展廳，則通過安全帽、BP機、情書、電話卡等農民工實物，還原了農民工生活的方方面面。

在四層展廳遊覽結束後，場館還設置了互動平台，參觀者可選擇裝修工、服務員、送水工、清潔工四個農民工工種進行電腦拍照，角色扮演，並可將照片通過網絡發往自己郵箱，過一把農民工癮。農民工博物館的構想，旨在紀念廣大農民工為廣東改革開放和現代化建設做出的突出貢獻，希望通過梳理和記錄這些歷史印記，提醒大家不忘農民工，善待農民工。「來廣州十年，我真正體會到了所有夢想都開花，農民工博物館這種形式極具人文關懷，充分肯定了農民工個體、群體的存在意義。」農民工詩人黃劍豐說。

國家人口計畫生育委員會流動人口服務管理司發布的《中國流動人口發展狀況報告》顯示，流動人口中 78.7％ 為農業戶口，以青壯年為主，十四歲及以下兒童占 20.8％，男性占 50.4％，女性占 49.6％。流動人口家庭平均規模為 2.3 人；十六歲至五十九歲人口中 86.8％ 接受過初中教育，人口月平均收入一九四二元人民幣。數據還顯示，中國流動人口平均在流入地停留超過五年。全國流動人口的平均年齡為 27.3 歲。這說明，大部分流動人員處於人生精力最充沛、思維最活躍的「黃金十年」中。他們有足夠的能力進行再學習、再深造。從頂層設計上，為這些人的「向上流動」助力，是廣東這些年一直在做的事情。社會各界對流動人員的激勵、關注以及力促改變的措施越來越多。

二〇一〇年十二月，共青團廣東省委聯合北京大學等相關單位啟動「圓夢計畫北大 100」項目，從報名的二千五百零一名新生代產業工人中遴選出一百位優秀分子，全額資助他們攻讀北京大學網絡遠程教育本科學位。

湖北青年潘焰出生在一個農民家庭，自記事起，家裡就很窮。鋤田耕地，播種收割，挑水施肥，便是他童年最主要的記憶。全家的收入來源於那幾畝農田，父母披星戴月地勞作，但生活也沒有因此有所改善。碰到旱澇天災，顆粒無收，家裡的口糧也就斷了。向鄰居借，向親戚借，沒有接濟根本維持不了生計。

曾經決心用「知識改變命運」的他，迫於家境貧困，初中畢業後，只報了中專。冀望兩年就能拿個文憑，又能學到一技之長，早點出來工作還可以幫補家用。畢業那年，恰逢國家出新政，中專生也可以參加高考。潘焰以全校第二的成績考上了武漢的一所大專院校，終於如願考上了大學！在親朋好友的幫助下，湊齊了第一年的學費，圓了大學夢。

　　大學期間，幾乎所有寒暑假潘焰都在外兼職：當過網吧的網管，也做過工地的小工。記憶最深刻的是一年暑假，他在供電局做小工。近 40°C 的高溫下，背著沉重的電纜，攀爬一座座塔架，只為每天的二十塊工錢。電纜粗長而厚重，但沒有機器，全靠人力從一個塔架拉到另一個塔架。他每天都全身痠痛，手掌腳板也都磨起了泡。舊傷未好新傷又添，倍感力不從心而使不上勁，工作效率也就低了。工頭看了便大聲地吼：「你到底行不行啊？不行的話，明天就別來了！礙手礙腳的……」後來總算撐到了假期結束。大二下學期，潘焰去開發區面試一個 IT 實習生的職位。因中專大學都是學計算機，專業知識和技能水平都不差，他很順利就被錄取了。一星期兩天班，一天就有六十塊。從那時候起，他再也沒有向家裡要生活費了。

　　二〇〇六年，潘焰來到了深圳，在一家外語培訓機構當工程師。工作之餘，他堅持學習，終於在二〇〇八年考過了思科認證；二〇〇九年拿到了微軟認證。職位也從原來的工程師升到了主管，再到華南區 IT 經理的位置。在人才輩出且競爭激烈的深圳，大專學歷到底是潘焰心頭的一塊硬傷。二〇一一年初，在報紙上看到共青團廣東省委實施「圓夢計畫北大 100」，資助新生代產業工人讀大學這個消息，他喜出望外。網上報名，現場確認，複習備考，終於成為了「圓夢計畫」的一員。

在圓夢計畫的學習裡，潘焰通過了英語和計算機的統考，也通過了北京地區學位英語考試；畢業論文達到了申請學位的分數。二〇一五年四月，通過獵頭公司的介紹，潘焰跳槽到一家企業，並拿到了年薪三十萬元的職位。

從二〇一〇年「北大100」的播種試水，到二〇一一年百個「圓夢100」的推廣灌溉，再到目前六萬名新生代產業工人的幸福花開，「圓夢計畫」項目一路前行，不斷壯大，規模已接近一所真正意義上的大學。二〇一六年，是「圓夢計畫」骨幹學員交流營活動舉辦的第四個年頭，截至年底，廣東累計培訓圓夢學員骨幹人數超過八千人。

留在父母身邊

目前中國共有 610.55 萬的留守兒童，長期過著沒有父母相陪的「一個人」生活。而湮沒在歷史時光中的留守者，至少有整整一代人。和父母在一起，這是 6100 萬農村留守兒童樸實而奢侈的願望。兒童不再留守，就是要讓他們與父母團聚。讓父母返鄉，還是讓孩子隨遷？學者段成榮的建議是，從制度上創造條件，讓孩子跟著父母進城。

二〇一六年，是廣東全面放開異地高考的首年，共有九千五百多名外省戶籍隨遷子女考生報名在廣東參加高考。而在廣州，有一千零五十六名外省戶籍隨遷子女得以留下來參加高考。二〇一六年六月六日晚，韓珺如在家裡吃完晚飯，坐上爸爸的車，返回北大為明實驗學校。老韓一家從山東臨沂來廣州，已有十四年，早已適應了廣州的飲食，尤其是韓珺如，四五歲時隨父母南下，活脫脫的一個廣州姑娘。韓太太入鄉隨俗，煲得一手好湯，這天晚上煲的紅棗烏雞，益氣補血，是女兒最愛喝的湯。「如果不是異地高考，或許現在我們全家都已經搬回臨沂了。無論如何，我都不能讓女兒成為『留守兒童』。」老韓說。他在廣州從事紡織生意，經過十多年的打拼，如今已是有車有房，兒女雙全，在廣州站穩了腳跟，但直到去年十二月以前，女兒的高考問題都是老韓的心病。女兒初三畢業的時候，夫妻倆帶著孩子回了一趟老家，見了老韓中學的班主任。「談得最多的就是女兒的教育問題，那時候廣東還是自主命題，跟山東用的不是同一套卷子，異地高考的政策雖然已經出台，但我們也擔心會不會有什麼變數。老師的建議是，讓孩子回山東念高中。」老韓說。與老韓同樣糾結的，還有來自廣西柳州的老張。一九九七年，他放棄了國企的工作，與妻子來到廣州打拚，女兒張綺夢一九九八年在廣州出生，可謂是土生土長。但因為父母戶籍不在廣州，綺夢在讀書問題上沒少折騰。二〇一〇年，綺夢過五關斬六將，考進了民辦的天河省實附中。「我們當時挺矛盾的，曾經考慮過將孩子送回去廣西，讓爺爺奶奶照顧，以後留在老家參加高考，這樣教育經費也能省下好多。」老張說。然而最終，老韓和老張都決定讓孩子留在廣州念書，「不能讓孩子成為留守兒童」是他們共同的想法。「如果女兒要回去念高中，她的媽媽肯定要回去陪讀的。一家人不可能長期兩地分居，或許過個一兩年，我也會結束在廣州的生意，回臨沂重新開始。」老韓說。

韓珺如和張綺夢都是住校生，每週末回家。巧的是，兩人各自有一個九歲的弟弟。高考前在家裡待的最後一晚，珺如破天荒看了電視。為了給女兒減壓，老韓特意為她在 ipad 上下載了電影《瘋狂動物城》。兩個考生的弟弟都非常懂事，珺如的弟弟在姐姐回家的時候，從不嚷著看電視，總是安靜地躲在角落裡看書寫作業，或者進房間裡打遊戲。「我希望未來有更多隨遷子女能夠受益於異地高考，更希望隨遷子女能夠享受到更多與戶籍生同等的受教育機會。尤其是近年中考，非戶籍生上公辦高中的競爭一直非常激烈，希望到小兒子中考、高考的時候，他能成為受益者。」老韓說。

在廣州，來穗人員子女教育問題一直引人注目。據統計，僅二〇一三年，廣州就有二十三萬非戶籍學生在公辦學校就讀，占非戶籍學生總數 42%。二〇一六年九月，市政府常務會議審議通過了

《關於進一步做好來穗人員隨遷子女接受義務教育工作的實施意見》，明確凡持有在廣州辦理廣東省居住證滿一年的來穗人員，可向所在區為子女申請積分入學。作為多年的教育強區，在此次方案裡，越秀區提出，在學前教育階段，凡符合條件的來穗人員適齡子女與戶籍適齡兒童同等享受區屬公辦幼兒園電腦搖號資格；義務教育階段，面向符合條件的來穗人員隨遷適齡子女免費提供義務教育公辦學校學位。番禺區提出，二〇一六年起啟動向民辦學校購買學位實施辦法，進一步增加免費學位數量，到二〇二〇年實現符合條件的非戶籍常住人口子女接受義務教育與當地戶籍學生享有同等待遇。同時力促民辦學校規范、優質、特色、持續發展，為來穗人員子女入學提供多元選擇。

在深圳，二〇一五年的義務教育滿意度調查顯示，非深圳戶口家長對深圳教育滿意度高於深圳戶口家長。深圳市教育局負責人表示，這說明深圳充分發揮公辦學校在解決外來工子女入學中的主渠道作用。深圳在義務教育均衡、公平方面受到家長認可。在深圳二〇一四年義務教育階段新生招生 25.4 萬人中，共有 17.7 萬人屬於非深戶籍學生，占比達到 69.7%，無論是小一還是初一，非深戶籍學生都超過了六成以上。按照這樣的比例，作為一線城市的深圳在解決外來人口的上學方面保持了最大的開放態度。作為擁有眾多外來務工者的大城市，深圳從二〇一四年起，在國內率先全面推行積分入學辦法，保障了外來人口子女的就讀需求。非深戶入學需要用到「1+5」政策，根據政策，凡年滿六到十五週歲，有學習能力，父母在深連續居住一年以上（居住證、社保、房產證或租賃合同有一項超過一年即滿足此條件）即可申請在深圳接受義務教育。深圳市教育局的一名官員表示，國家在逐漸淡化戶籍概念，深圳目前實行的「積分入學」政策，可以讓戶籍和非戶籍人口在同一起跑線上，有相對平等的機會。

我在這裡
挺好的

郝蓮露：洋媳婦在廣州

二〇一六年七月，廣州著名本土劇《外來媳婦本地郎》突破了三千集。這是中國電視史上播出時間最久、播出集數最多、同時段同類型節目收視率最高、影響力最廣、經濟效益最好的電視系列情景劇。

在劇中，康家老四阿祖的老婆戴安娜，是廣東一所私立中學的英語老師。這名來自美國的洋美女，是昌盛街最耀眼的「外來媳婦」。受過良好的教育，性格簡單直接，原則性強，凡事也容易較真，主動參與家庭事務與街道的公益事業，可惜因文化差異，有時與丈夫、公婆妯娌之間也有「水土不服」的矛盾。最突出的性格特點就是認死理，守規矩。從某種程度上說，戴安娜的故事，是扮演者郝蓮露的真實寫照。這名來自德國的高知美女，因為出演《外來媳婦本地郎》一劇，已經成為廣州著名的外國人之一。

郝蓮露出生在德國慕尼黑市一個知識分子家庭，一九九二年，她從慕尼黑大學漢學系畢業後來到北京大學留學。一九九三年底，著名表演藝術家丁廣泉有個小品缺一個外國女演員，這時，北大老師向他推薦了郝蓮露。雙方見面後，丁老師覺得郝蓮露很有喜劇天賦，而且不怯場，對她很滿意，當即決定由她出演那個角色，並收她為洋徒弟。就這樣，郝蓮露成為了著名洋笑星——加拿大人「大山」的師妹。她曾榮獲外國人中華才藝大賽一等獎，多次參加中央電視台主辦的大型文藝演出，表演的《洋腔洋調》《賽戲招婿》《駱駝祥子》等小品風靡一時。不僅如此，她還先後在中央電視台、廣東電視台和澳門衛視主持過節目，並主演了《外來媳婦本地郎》《阮愛國在香港》等多部影視劇，是外國藝人中在中國發展最好的女笑星。在北大求學期間，郝蓮露認識了「老北京」王宏業。一九九五年初，兩人舉行了婚禮。後來，為了事業上的發展，郝蓮露選擇獨自南下到廣東主持一檔旅遊節目，不久憑藉一口「洋粵語」，成為《外來媳婦本地郎》的演員，丈夫則留守北京。幾年後，王宏業追隨妻子的腳步來到廣州。從此，這一對「外來媳婦北京郎」，成為了長居淘金路的廣州街坊。

郝蓮露的性格里，有著德國人特有的執拗。《外來媳婦本地郎》劇中飾演老三的彭新智說，郝蓮露是典型的德國人性格，生活裡一切都安排得井井有條。「看她的車子裡就知道，收拾得很整齊。」另外，郝蓮露的認真個性還體現在對劇本「忠實」上。彭新智說：「我們很多戲是演員在劇本基礎上再互相商量出來的，但她就不習慣這種做法，一定要按照劇本來演。不過後來她慢慢受我們影響，懂得一點變通了。」

《外來媳婦本地郎》從二〇〇〇年十一月首播，至今已經播出快十七年了。郝蓮露在裡面的戲份不多。她已經不記得自己上一次拍戲是什麼時候，也不知道下一次入戲是什麼時候，一切都等待劇組的安排。儘管在戲裡，郝蓮露飾演的戴安娜是一個咋咋呼呼，很熱鬧的人，但現實中的郝蓮露卻十分安靜。據廣州某電視頻道編導回憶，劇組裡一般都是吵吵鬧鬧，各忙各的，身材高大的郝蓮露則喜歡窩在角落裡靜靜地看書，不管環境多麼嘈雜，她頭也不抬。在《外地媳婦本地郎》最火的那幾年裡，郝蓮露收到各種片約，演出、活動主持的工作不斷，但幾乎沒有哪個是她自己爭取的，基本上都是別人「找上門」。「有人請我，我就去，沒人請我，我就不去。我演也煩惱，不演也煩惱。」她對拍戲這件事情沒有追求，「隨便」是她的口頭禪。

其中最為人關注的細節是，作為一名北大畢業的「學霸」、古漢語專業的碩士，她現在是一名全職太太，在家教育兩個孩子。對於教育，郝蓮露有著自己的看法。有些大學畢業生，連換燈泡都不會，這讓她感到不可思議。

她也考察過國內的學校，但她並不認可。在她看來，一個班級的老師，面對著四五十名學生，與家長的溝通也極其有限。孩子一天至少有八小時在學校裡，除去做作業、睡覺的時間，一天中能和父母溝通交流的時間所剩無幾了。家長根本不知道孩子在學校學了什麼，說什麼，想什麼，這樣不行。因此，郝蓮露的兩個孩子，都沒有上學，而是留在家裡，由媽媽教育。來自德國的北大高材生的教育方法並沒有什麼特別之處，就是跟孩子交流，講背景和內容，跟著書本學，在生活中學，通過做手工也可以學。郝蓮露在北京的公公婆婆很不理解。在中國，許多父母為了孩子上個好學校，不惜花幾百萬元買學位房，就是為了進一所大眾眼裡的好學校。這個洋媳婦倒好，也不是讀不起好學校，偏要關起門來自己教。孩子在家學習這件事情上，郝蓮露又一次顯示了德國人的執拗：這件事情沒得商量。「從早上八點到下午五點，孩子們被圈在一塊，灌輸觀念和知識，只是教他們某個看問題的視角，該這樣或那樣看待事物，乖乖地，成績就好，沒有時間去思考真相，放學後頭腦裡一團亂麻。幾百年前，那時候沒有學校，大家都是在家裡上學，為什麼現在不可以？這是一個新的時代，我們需要頭腦風暴。你覺得不正常的事情，在別的文化圈，別的時代，完全可能是主流。」郝露蓮態度堅決，老人家無可奈何，也就聽之任之了。

在廣州居住了十多年後，郝蓮露已經完全融入了這座城市，關心廣州的建設。廣州大力推行垃圾分類之時，郝蓮露接受了媒體的採訪，分享了自己為垃圾進行分類的經驗。郝蓮露注意到，在同一棟樓裡，除了她自己，大部分鄰居都不太注重垃圾分類。「我經常聽到朋友跟我抱怨『家裡每天垃圾都好大一堆啊』，我都會跟他們說，如果你把能夠回收的部分分揀出來，這部分其實不是每天都要扔的，那麼剩下的其實沒多少。」郝蓮露介紹，在家裡，自己會把衛生間垃圾、塑料製品和玻璃瓶單獨分開放，另外還有紙類也是將它們壓平、疊好放在一起。分成幾類存放在廚房裡，積累到一定量就找收廢品的人上來收購。剩下的，就只有每天都會產生一點的廚餘垃圾了，看似毫無用處，郝蓮露卻對這些垃圾痛惜得很：「在德國幾乎每家都有個小花園，這些有機垃圾就是上好的花園肥料啊，多麼寶貴。在廣州只能扔掉了，太可惜了！」

馬特：洋女婿在廣州

「你好，我叫馬特！」英國人馬特與中國朋友們第一次見面時，總會這樣熱情地自我介紹。他的這句話說得字正腔圓，毫不費力，可當你期待著他進一步用流利的中文與你「侃大山」時，不可避免要失望了。這幾乎是他唯一會說的一句中文。這個魁梧英俊的英國男人旅居中國九年，在幼兒園裡教孩子們說英文，自己卻總也學不會中文。

馬特是一名幼兒園老師，許多人聽說這個職業後，都會顯得有些吃驚。事實上，馬特更像平面模特、健身教練或者企業高管。身材魁梧的他像一具莊嚴的古希臘雕塑──深陷的眼窩，高高的鼻樑，得體的著裝凸顯了他英國紳士的氣質。但熟悉他的人，會知道幼兒園老師對於他來說實在是太適合不過的工作了。他親切、幽默、面部表情豐富，模仿起人來也惟妙惟肖，英國人特有的幽默感讓他十分討人喜歡。哪怕很多時候，對方領悟不到言語中的笑點，也會被他的表情逗樂。

來中國前，馬特在英國是一名建築公司的採購員，簡單地說，就是從事室內裝潢的「買買買」工作。二〇〇八年經濟危機，英國經濟蕭條，大多數人面臨失業，馬特也沒能倖免。被裹挾在了失業的洪流中，他的無力感遠遠大於挫敗感。馬特並不認為是自己不夠好，而是經濟環境就是如此。他感覺自己也沒辦法迅速「打雞血」，重新找工作。於是，在商海中撲騰得有些精疲力盡，終於被拍上了沙灘的他，決定好好休息一段時間。他決定給自己放一個長假，但不是吃吃喝喝，遊山玩水，而是做一些自己覺得有意義的，真正喜歡的事情。一次偶然的機會，馬特得知有一個志願活動，是去中國的小村莊裡，教孩子們學英語。一個神祕的東方國度、靜謐的山村、孩子們純真的笑容，當這樣的畫面在馬特腦海中形成時，他便有了一拍大腿的衝動。「這不正是我想要的麼？」他興沖沖地報名參加了這個為期六週的志願者活動，來到了中國。只是，那時候的他，完全沒想到，自己的人生，從此換了軌道，他與中國的緣分，不是六週，而是九年甚至更長。

馬特和朋友們來到廣西桂林陽朔。宋嘉泰元年（西元 1201 年），廣南西路提點刑獄公事王正功作詩云：「桂林山水甲天下，玉碧羅青意可參。」此後，「桂林山水甲天下」便成為了中國流傳最久遠、範圍最廣的旅遊廣告語。桂林作為中國首批對外開放的旅游城市之一，同時也是國內最早接待入境遊客的五城市（北京、西安、上海、桂林、廣州）之一，在一九七二年就開始接待外國國家元首。四十多年來，桂林不僅成為境外遊客熟知的旅遊目的地，境外遊客量也一直位居全國地級城市前茅。作為陽朔縣城內最古老的街道——西街，被戲稱為全中國最大的「英語角」。每年來這裡居住、休閒的外國人相當於這裡常住人口的三倍。

初來乍到的隔閡很快隨著志願工作的深入而消解，馬特他們在晚上常被邀請到村民們的家裡做客。即使語言不通，但大家坐在一起，用肢體語言或者畫畫來交流。孩子們最喜歡的事情就是圍著四個老外問各種各樣的問題。他們捧著書本，指著上面的英國圖案很興奮地問：「你是來自那裡嗎？」清澈的眼睛裡寫滿了好奇，讓馬特動容。「當個老師，似乎還不錯！」種子從此在馬特心裡種下。

六週的志願活動結束後，馬特不想離開了。在預計本應到達英國的星期二那天，他跟他的朋友們通了個電話：「我不回去了，我決定留在中國。」

　　「你瘋了嗎？你在中國什麼都沒有！」

　　「英國沒有足以呼喚我回去的東西。」

　　馬特留在了中國。在志願者項目負責人的幫助下，他來到了廣州。到達廣州那天是一個週日，陽光很好。如果說，山清水秀的陽朔帶給馬特的是震撼以及好奇，那麼大都市廣州則讓馬特感到既熟悉又陌生。什麼都能吃到、什麼都能看到、什麼都能買到。只要找到一份工作，就可以在這裡過得很好，和在英國的時候一樣。第二天一早他便被通知去幼兒園面試英語教師，並且順利地得到了這份工作。九年了，他還在做著這份工作。馬特的母親是一名教師，她曾在馬特十八歲時問過他和弟弟以後要不要像她一樣成為一名教師，當時他和弟弟都斬釘截鐵地拒絕了母親的提議，為此她還失落了一會。然而，彷彿是宿命，馬特在命運的拐角處走出，毫無徵兆地一腳跨上了教壇，實現了母親的願望。更有意思的是，馬特的弟弟在澳大利亞，同樣是一名英語老師。

　　馬特在廣州結識的第一個新朋友，便是他後來的妻子。來到廣州三天后，他路過廣州圖書館舊館，發現廣場上聚了一群人，有中國人還有外國人，好奇心驅使他上前一探究竟，原來是個「英語角」。從上個世紀九〇年代開始，中國城市裡開始出現三種英語口語交流活動，分別是：英語角、英語沙龍和英語派對。在廣州，有四大「英語角」，廣州圖書館舊館便是其中之一。每週日上午，在百年大榕樹前的空地上，各類英語愛好者便會聚在一起，用英語談天說地。有人說，「英語角」在中國，同時也是婚姻介紹所，許多美麗的愛情故事從此展開，馬特親身驗證了其真實性。有一天，在人群中，一個甜美的女生朝馬特走來，寒暄了幾句後，兩人在附近找了個地方坐下，開始有一搭沒一搭地閒聊。對於聊了些什麼，馬特已經記不清楚了，只記得整個過程讓他感到非常愉悅。兩個成長環境迥異的年輕人，卻有著非常多的共同話題，同時又對彼此的生活充滿了好奇。他們就這麼聊著、笑著，一見如故。姑娘的笑容很美，幾乎要把馬特融化，他那一刻的心情，就如同姑娘的容顏一般美好。馬特禮貌地向女生索要聯繫方式，卻遭到了拒絕。「好吧，這是東方人特有的謹慎和含蓄。」馬特並未感到挫敗。他們相約了下一次英語角活動，幾次見面後，兩人成了朋友，姑娘幫馬特找房子，帶他熟悉廣州，他們一起吃飯，時常見面，電話號碼自然是拿到了，後來，他們順理成章地相愛了，並最終修成正果結為夫妻。

馬特眼中的妻子既像小孩子一樣可愛，會因為學會了一道菜而開心很久，又是一個優雅有主見的女強人。只是偶爾，他會覺得妻子活得太累，太不恣意。工作那麼多，卻不敢跟老闆提意見。馬特的妻子在一家英語培訓機構工作，剛開始的工作是秘書，後來老闆發現她英語不錯，就讓她去當英語老師，不久又發現她電腦技術也不錯，她又要去教別人電腦。每一次轉變，都是老闆安排的，妻子並沒有什麼話語權，只能服從。除了本職工作，她還要做很多雜七雜八的事情，許多工作都是在職責範圍之外的。在英國，員工如果覺得老闆安排不合理，都會提出來，或者跟老闆談條件。但中國的員工大多聽話，不敢表達不滿。這在馬特看來，是因為中國人太多了，職場競爭壓力太大。馬特勸說過妻子多次，讓她學會說

「NO」，妻子嘴上抱怨，行動上卻始終兢兢業業。久而久之，馬特習慣了，也理解了妻子的身不由己。妻子偶爾抱怨時，他更多的是安慰、擁抱，讓她有一個發洩的出口。

中國女性勤儉持家的美德，在英國洋女婿看來，也是有些太委屈自己。馬特的妻子總會因為自己喜歡的東西貴而猶豫很久。馬特卻認為買喜歡的東西是一件很棒的事情，所以總會在一旁勸，簡直比推銷員還賣力。但多數情況下，妻子還是會扭頭走掉。有好幾次，馬特偷偷買回去送給她的時候，她都會嗔怪太浪費錢，可還是會忍不住開心地笑。馬特總是給妻子「洗腦」：「你要關注的是自己真正喜歡的東西，而不是錢。」

當了九年的廣州街坊，馬特至今卻不會說中文。剛到廣州時，他也去上過中文班，可最終卻堅持不下去。馬特並不認為是自己的原因，而是這些中文班所教的東西，並不是他真正想要的。馬特更希望學到日常用語，知道要怎麼叫出租車，到銀行要講什麼，但中文學校的老師們更喜歡教『bpmf』之類。馬特感到枯燥乏味，雖然他也認可從基礎學起，但並不打算花那麼多的時間去學如何說得字正腔圓，語法精確。就像很多到英國去的外國人一樣，他們沒有系統地學過英語，但也能在那裡生活幾十年。幸運的是，不會說中文這件事，對馬特的生活並沒有造成太大的影響。在廣州，基本上任何一個年齡段的人都會說基礎的英語。比如在餐廳，大多數服務員都會說英語，馬特用英文點餐，服務員並不會出現一頭霧水的神情。他也可以用英文向的士司機說明目的地。遇上有司機繞路時，他還會提醒司機，「嘿朋友你走遠嘍！我認識路的！」他甚至認為粵語比普通話好學一點，廣東話有九個不同的聲調，講起來像唱歌一樣，很有律動性。儘管沒有足夠的動力和毅力去學習中文，但馬特卻始終對不會說中文這件事耿耿於懷，原因是他總是為此遭到妻子無情的「嘲笑」。為了證明自己，他曾經想把心一橫，到中國的某個不那麼國際化的小城市裡待上一兩年，逼迫自己泡在中文環境裡，回來向妻子炫耀一口流利的中文。

如今，馬特和太太有了一個五歲的小男孩，名叫奧斯汀。在這個英國男人與中國之間，已經有了血脈連接。小人兒永遠坐不住，即使在大雨天也想跑出去玩。也許遺傳了英國人的體質，當他的中國同學都穿上了大衣的時候，他還只穿一件 T 恤。這讓馬特和太太感到費腦筋，每天早上都要和他「搏鬥」好一會兒，才能讓他穿多一件衣服。正是應了那句「青出於藍而勝於藍」，與學不會中文的馬特相比，奧斯汀的語言天賦實在是太好了，小小年紀就能說普通話、粵語、英語三種語言。在幼兒園、外婆和媽媽以及爸爸之間無障礙地進行語言切換。

與郝蓮露一樣，馬特對中國教育也形成了自己的想法。大部分家長對他畢恭畢敬的態度，讓他頗有些無所適從。中國學校給他的感受是，meeting 意味著家長們坐在下面認真地聽老師講話。這時候的老師更像是一個老闆，點評每一個孩子，乃至家長：「你這個做得很好，那個做錯了，以後不能再犯。」家長不停點頭，卻不發言，老師把話說完了，然後就散會。作為一個外國人，他其實很想改變這種現狀，想在 meeting 的時候和家長一起討論問題，討論怎樣讓學生或讓學校變得更好，而不是老師們一味地講，家長們一味地點頭，但收效不大。就好比一場晚會，導演不斷地熱場，讓觀眾們「high」起來，但觀眾的表現卻始終很木然，甚至只是在欣賞著導演一個人的表演。久而久之，馬特也不再強求了，他再度把這種差別歸因於「文化」。不僅家長聽話，學生們也特別乖，在中國當老師特別有權威性。如果有學生不聽話，你只要跟他說「我可能會想找你的父母談一談」，學生們立馬乖乖聽話。如果在英國，學生會自己撥通電話「媽媽，我們老師想找你談一談」，然後將電話遞給老師，另一隻手繼續著他正在玩的遊戲。

　　一個在倫敦工作生活了很多年的英國人，說他最愛廣州的天氣和食物，相信沒有人會感到意外。久居廣州的馬特，為了保持身材，付出了巨大的努力。當面對琳瑯滿目的食品，他的選擇只有兩條——控制住少吃，或者吃完之後拚命運動。馬特無法抵禦食物的誘惑力，他毫不猶豫地選擇了後者。他願意為了食物和身材，付出更多的汗水。在英國，馬特煩惱的是，有什麼可吃的。在廣州，他的煩惱走向了另一個極端：選擇困難症，不知道該吃什麼。他所迷戀的，不僅僅是本土粵菜，而是能在廣州吃到的世界各地的美食。但和許多外國人一樣，馬特有一張食品黑名單，讓廣州人食指大動的鳳爪，他就望而生畏。在一趟列車上，他第一次見到有人吃雞爪。坐在對面的男生，投入、忘我地抓著一隻雞爪啃，彷彿整個世界，除了雞爪，一切都不重要了。馬特呆呆地看了許久，男生那滿足的神情深深地烙在了他的記憶裡。後來在太太的「逼迫」下，馬特嘗試過雞爪，奇怪的筋絡和骨骼以及前所未有的口感，讓他發誓再也不碰這東西。有意思的是，奧斯汀特別喜歡吃雞爪。有一次，馬特帶著他和妻子回到英國，與朋友聚會的過程中，奧斯汀突然跟媽媽說：「我要吃雞爪！」周圍的人全都吃驚地瞪大了眼睛，彷彿在看一個小怪物。中西飲食文化的碰撞以如此戲劇性又生活化的方式展現出來，讓馬特感到特別有意思。

如今的馬特，已經完全融入了廣州的生活，成為了一名普通廣州街坊。他喜歡在夜晚和朋友們聚在一起享受美食，飯後散散步，聊聊天，享受一下或溫暖或涼爽的天氣，感覺特別愜意。他生活中的一大樂趣，便是看英國老家的天氣預報，然後把兩地的天氣預報截個圖，通過社交軟件發給英國朋友們，嘲笑一番：「哈哈哈哈！真可憐，你們那裡看起來真冷！看到沒有，我在冬天只用穿兩件！」

馬特會過每一個「洋節」，也會過中國傳統節日。每年聖誕節，馬特都是幼兒園裡最受歡迎的人。因為他會化身成聖誕老公公，給孩子們派發禮物。一些眼尖的小朋友會認出馬特，他們會興奮地尖叫，咯咯笑著爬到馬特身上，扯他的鬍子。對於中國的春節，馬特則顯得不那麼「感冒」。但一年一度的人口大遷徙——春運，則讓他感到震驚不已。人們就像候鳥一樣，在春節前湧向機場、火車站、汽車站，短短幾天裡，城市幾乎空了。一週後，城市又再度被人填滿了。馬特也希望在春節期間，進入遷徙者的隊伍裡。他心目中理想的春節假期，是可以飛到澳大利亞探望弟弟，順便在溫暖的南半球享受一個有陽光、海灘相伴的假期。只是，大多數年份裡，他都要陪妻子留在廣州與家人團聚。除夕團聚讓馬特真切感受到中國人對家庭的重視，但在熱鬧的氛圍中，他卻有些寂寞。一屋子十多口人，都用中文交流。妻子無暇翻譯，多數時間裡，馬克只能在一旁陪笑。親戚家的孩子們看到馬特卻是異常興奮，總是拉著他出去玩。於是，馬特不得不繼續當「孩子王」。

廣州一直被譽為中國最宜居的城市之一。有時候，她像一個大家閨秀，隨時都可以濃墨重彩，閃亮登場。有時候，又婉約如小家碧玉，嬌羞地等待著別人來發現她的美好。一個充滿了市民氣息的國際化大都市，不同的人，以不同的方式生活於此，都能找到屬於自己的快樂。對於馬特來說，喜歡這座城，更多地是因為這裡的人。他形容自己去過的一些大城市，那裡的人步伐匆匆，忙著賺錢。就算你在他們面前擺成一個「大」字大喊「Hello!」都不一定有人理睬。相比之下，廣州人性情溫和，也更樂於助人，廣州人讓廣州成為一座有溫度的城市。

對於英國，馬特依然有眷戀，他每年會回去英國兩次。與父母親友團聚。但待的時間長了，他又覺得有點無聊了。他已經習慣了在廣州的生活，回去反而不太適應英國的氣候。在寒冷的冬天裡，他只能百無聊賴地坐在屋子裡，看著窗外的雨瑟瑟發抖。網上社交圈也讓他感覺，與朋友們即使久別重逢，想說的話似乎卻沒有多少。大家說的無非就是「房子裝修了」「買了新車」，而這些事情，馬特早已在他們網上社交圈看過了，沒什麼新鮮的。

二〇一五年，馬特坐上開往陽朔的高鐵，回到了八年前的小村莊。那是他踏上的第一片中國的土地，也是讓他愛上並留在中國的地方。他行走在路上——那段他曾幫忙鋪過的路——人們已不再訝異於他的淺色瞳孔；購物於商城，亦再無他人的新奇目光。彼物已改，彼景亦換，彼人或離，此情猶在。若陽朔於馬特，是初戀，那麼廣州便是將與其偕老的妻子。九年來，他經歷了廣州太多的變遷，陪伴著廣州日新月異，廣州見證著他堅守初心，兩者已不可分離。

▎擁抱洋鄰居：服務就在身邊

　　廣州警方最新統計數據顯示，廣州日常在住外國人數量約八萬，最多時接近十二萬；外國人在住數排在前五位的國家分別是韓國、日本、美國、印度、加拿大。郝蓮露與馬特在廣州的生活，是「外國人在廣州的縮影」。如今，在廣州居住的外國人，在地理上基本上形成幾大中心：以環市東路為中心的秀山樓、淘金路、花園酒店、建設六馬路、建設大馬路等一帶，以一些從事貿易的非洲人和歐洲國家領事館、日本領事館為主；

　　以天河北路為中心的體育東、天河路、龍口西路、林和中路等一帶，因中信廣場內有大量的外國公司辦事處，所以大部分從事貿易的日本人、美洲人、歐洲人都居住在附近；

　　番禺區一些大型、配套設施較好的樓盤如祈福新村、麗江花園一帶，主要以東亞地區和東南亞地區國家如日本、泰國、馬來西亞等國人居多；

　　還有以三元裡為中心的白雲區金桂村、機場路小區等地，這裡主要是經營鞋類、服裝生意的非洲人居住，近年來不少從事中韓貿易的韓國人也聚集在此；

　　而在天河北路芳草園，外國住戶分別來自沙特阿拉伯、伊朗、土耳其、英國、日本、韓國等國家。

　　越秀區的天秀大廈則以非洲人和中東人商戶居多。天秀大廈六百多間寫字樓中，有七成是被中東人和非洲人租用。他們開的商店，多以銷售日用百貨、服裝、鞋帽、紡織品為主，甚至還有縫紉機、馬燈等國人已少見的商品。

《南方日報》的一項調查顯示，以十分製為城市印象分的滿分對廣州進行評價，百分之四十二的外國友人分值在八分以上。大部分外國友人認為，老廣對待老外比較淡定。來自美國的 Chad 說，北京人對外國人非常熱情，甚至會邀請外國人到家裡吃飯，上海人會把外國當作目標，「人們總想從你身上得到什麼」，而在江西九江，家長帶著小孩看到外國人時會慫恿孩子「去跟他練習英語吧」。在廣州，當 Chad 隨著人流走出地鐵時，他會意識到自己是廣州的一位市民，在廣州並沒有招來過多的關注，「我覺得可以用『不在意』來形容廣州人對外國人的態度」。

儘管表面上淡定，但廣州這座低調務實，做得多說得少的城市，近年來一直致力於外國人服務管理方面的創新，以求讓老外們在廣州過得更舒心和更安心，同時儘可能為在廣州逗留的外國人提供最大的便利。

二〇一三年六月十四日，在失聯了一個多月後，俄羅斯姑娘阿斯塔菲娃‧尤莉婭（ASTAFYEVA YULIA）終於見到了母親。阿斯塔菲娃‧尤莉婭二〇一三年三月乘火車從滿洲裡獨自入境，但六月份時突然與父母失去聯繫，身邊的朋友也不見了。人們再次發現她時，是在番禺洛浦街橘樹村的一個小士多里，身無分文，也沒有任何證件，手抓著一包香菸和一瓶礦泉水不放手。接到熱心市民報警後，警方決定將其暫時送到番禺區救助站，隨後又將其帶回洛浦街外國人管理服務工作站瞭解情況。工作站的工作人員在翻譯的幫助下，取得了阿斯塔菲娃‧尤莉婭母親的電話。從她母親口中得知，阿斯塔菲娃‧尤莉婭患有癲癇，不患病時一切都正常，此前一直與家裡有聯繫，但六月七日與家裡失去聯繫，估計是病情發作，家裡已及時向領事館報案。飛到廣州接回女兒後，阿斯塔菲婭·尤莉婭的母親向工作站人員以及番禺區各方面表達了由衷的感謝。救助阿斯塔菲婭·尤莉婭的番禺區洛浦街外國人管理服務工作站，成立於二〇〇八年，是廣州首個針對外國人管理服務而設立的社區工作站。有意在番禺洛溪板塊居住的所有外國人，不用跑很遠的路程，就可以在家門口辦理各種必要的住宿登記手續。與此同時，當地公安機關也可以就近為轄區內的外國人提供各種必要的上門管理服務。目前，廣州市所有外國人聚居超過二百人的鎮街，都已經像洛浦街道一樣，逐步成立專門的外國人管理服務社區工作站。

在廣州白雲區金沙街，隨著地鐵六號線開通，這裡與市區的交通越來越便利。目前，金沙街在住外國人六百零四人，同比增長了百分之九十一，來自八十多個國家和地區，其中以亞洲和非洲國家為主。隨著越來越多外國人來此生活居住，當地居民也時常感受著文化差異所帶來的問題。比如，外國人喜歡與友人在家裡聚會，而本地居民相對更喜歡清靜的生活。為了讓洋鄰居和街坊們相處更融洽，金沙街於二〇一五年九月建立了外國人管理服務工作站，並建立起一個以派出所為主導，街道辦、居委會、物業和相關職能部門一起參加的聯席會議機制，提高涉外工作效率和反應速度，實現外國人管理社會化。此外，金沙街還通過社會翻譯平台，聘請了社會翻譯參與外管工作，解決派出所日常工作中翻譯力量不足的問題，推進了「全警涉外」的警務理念。警方製作了中英文對照的涉外宣傳資料，在外管服務站放置了觸屏查詢一體機，裡面設置了金沙街的概況、辦理住宿登記的流程和辦理簽證服務指引等相關資料，方便外國人瞭解相關法律法規和辦證流程。金沙街派出所還建立了微信公眾號，外國人、出租屋主、房屋中介、物業公司只要掃瞄微信二維碼就可以進入派出所微信公眾號，收到各類涉外宣傳信息或溫馨提示等實時信息。

越秀區登峰街的寶漢地區，是廣州人口中知名的「非洲村」，因為全城五分之一的常住非洲人都聚居在這裡，規模逾千人。在高峰時期，加上短期住宿和商貿往來、探親訪友的非洲人，可以達到上萬人。為了幫助居住在此地的外國人解決生活中的難題，從而讓他們更好地融入到地區中來，街道的社工機構發放了二百多份問卷，而後再入戶探訪，從而針對外國人的需求推出了社區融入項目。「我們在調查中發現他們最大的需求就是語言學習問題，所以社區融入的第一步就是開辦中文學習班——『中文堂』，從週一到週六，從下午三點鐘上課到五點鐘。他們通過學習能掌握了一些日常生活中的漢語，幫助他們看病、換錢、問路，甚至是進行簡單的商貿。」廣州大學社會學系副教授、廣州市社會工作發展中心理事長王亮說。中文課堂上，來自五湖四海的同學們，都帶著自己的故事。無論是學生還是做生意的，無論家境貧困還是殷實，都從集體的相處中尋回了安全感和歸屬感。一些在本地生活時間較長、中文較好的外國人，還會在課餘、工餘時間自願到服務部來當義工，從服務對象反過來成為提供服務的人，幫助新來的外國人。為了實現服務「零距離」，越秀區還建立了面向外國人的互聯網互動平台，運用「證件通」信息採集設備，方便外國人就近辦理簽證延期申請等事務。

二〇一六年六月三十日，國際移民組織（IOM）舉行的特別理事會通過決議，批准中國正式成為國際移民組織成員國，開啟了中國參與國際移民合作的新篇章。廣州作為觀察中國移民管理的窗口，在外國人管理方面的創新實踐，贏得了國際移民組織的高度評價。

來了，
就不想離開

馬立安：我愛這土地愛得深沉

　　很多人愛深圳。愛她的日新月異、愛她的活力充沛、愛她狂奔向前的勁頭。而有一個美國女人，她對深圳的愛很是特別——她愛深圳的歷史、愛深圳的城中村。有人說深圳是「文化沙漠」，她卻一頭紮進「沙漠」中，一待就是二十一年，發現「沙漠」處處是綠洲。誰說深圳沒文化，她跟誰急。她叫馬立安，來自美國的人類學家，任職於香港浸會大學（深圳）。主要研究城中村歷史變遷，有關深圳「城中村」的各種會議、沙龍，基本上少不了她。

　　「你從哪裡來？」「你在哪裡結婚？」「你從哪兒去市場？」二〇一五年四月至十月，馬立安和同事付娜，帶著研究團隊，對深圳福田區十五個村子的老人進行口述歷史的蒐集。每一個人講述平凡人生，組成了一個關於城市的記憶。馬立安將蒐集到的「福田故事」製成圖示，邀請不同年齡層的市民參與創作。六個月的時間，馬立安和團隊走訪了福田區的十五個村子。跟村子裡的長者進行聊天式的採訪，在這個過程中，馬立安有許多有趣的發現。例如，作為國際化大都市，如今的深圳毋庸置疑已經是一座移民城市。在很多人的認知中，「國際化」「移民」這些詞彙與深圳扯上關係，都是改革開放之後的事情。但事實上，早在宋朝年間，便有移民遷徙而來。福田十五個村子有八大姓氏。其中，黃氏的祖先從河南經福建、江西等地來到下沙、上梅林、上沙和福田，在皇崗和水圍村有文天祥和莊子的後代。移民的匯聚也帶來了語言的融合和變遷。深圳本地至少有七種方言。龍崗、寶安說的是新安縣城官話，如今只有不到五千人會講；客家話是比較普及的一種方言；還有介於廣東話和客家話之間的圍頭話；大鵬話是所城駐軍的官方話；坪山的占米話，它是客家話的一個變化，但仍被語言學家認為是一個小方言；還有過去漁民們說的土語疍家話，這個方言跟深圳作為漁村有很大關係。直到上世紀九〇年代，北方移民成為主流，普通話才成為通用語言。而深圳的「國際化」，在馬立安看來，早在十九世紀，福田村裡的人們信奉媽祖，南山區的赤灣天后媽祖廟是海上絲綢之路很重要的一個停靠站。鄭和下西洋的時候曾經到過這裡。而事實上，福建、浙江、廣州等沿海地區都有拜媽祖的習俗。很多南方人將他們對媽祖的信仰帶到中國台灣、越南、日本和東南亞，今天大約有一千五百個媽祖廟分佈在二十六個國家。

作為二〇一五年深圳（福田）國際城區影像節的活動之一，馬立安在福田圖書館開設「福田故事：新家譜」公眾學堂。在一場新聞發布會上，馬立安的一口京腔，讓不少現場媒體都折服。她開設公眾學堂，是希望在深圳的新生代，能夠懂自己腳下的這片土地，因為瞭解，而與之發生連接。例如，讓一個十來歲的孩子，能夠在圖畫中找到自己的房子，能夠講自己的方言，告訴人們他們家的事情。他們在城市歷史中找到了自己與時空的聯繫。假如他們去日本，會發現日本有天后廟，而深圳也有天后廟，大家沒有血緣關係，語言不一樣，但是為什麼都會來拜天后？他們會提出和思考這些問題。讓年輕人思考這座城市的歷史，以及他與這座城市的聯結，便是馬立安的初衷所在。對於城市歷史的認知，對于歸屬感的尋求，並不是一次課就能解決。它是一個過程，而馬立安們所做的核心，就是在播撒種子。

早在小學六年級的時候，馬立安已與深圳結緣。學校讓孩子們做一份第三世界國家的報告，她選擇的主題恰好是中國。從此對這個國家產生了興趣。上高中時，馬立安曾赴菲律賓留學一年，住在當地的一個華僑家裡，接觸了中國的語言和文化。大學期間，她在中國台灣深入系統地學習了一年漢語，為中文能力打下基礎。一九九四年，還在休斯敦唸書的馬立安，因為中文好，接待了來自深圳的一個代表團。團裡的一個人說，可以幫她寫信介紹到深圳大學做人類學研究。

　　深圳和休斯敦是友好城市，但馬立安對深圳卻毫無概念。這份來自深圳的善意邀請，促使馬立安翻閱了有關深圳的資料。她大概瞭解到，休斯敦和深圳的發展策略很相似，當時他們都有海港和大的工業項目，休斯敦主要做石油，對空氣的污染很大。許多城市在發展時都是先關注經濟，到了一定階段才開始關注環保。她對深圳產生了興趣，想看看大洋彼岸這座陌生的城市，是否也循著同樣的路徑發展。一九九五年，做博士論文研究的馬立安，踏上了深圳的土地。在此之前，她已經去過北京、上海、廣州。而在美國，對中文或者漢學感興趣的人，首選地基本也是北上廣。馬立安到深圳時，很多朋友勸她去北京。在這個過程中，馬立安發現了一個有意思的事情：以前，人們對城市的自豪感還是來自於歷史和文化，而不是現代化。現在則完全不同。現在許多人開始為深圳感到自豪，覺得當時來深圳是對的，但那時候，深圳並不在大多數的人選擇名單內，當時他們覺得深圳是一個經濟的城市，不是文化的，覺得文化應該是在北京或者上海。正因為如此，歷史和現代化在深圳形成了有趣的碰撞，它既需要中國古老的文化和歷史，又希望成為像香港這樣的現代化城市，它希望將這兩樣組織起來。

初到深圳，馬立安住在當時深圳大學專為外國學生提供的潮汐樓，但每月五百美元的租金讓她不得不選擇逃離。幾番尋覓，她搬入深圳大學附近的粵海門村，不到六百元人民幣的租金讓她喜出望外。她落腳於此，並開始了訪問和調查研究。她成為了一名「城中村」居民，並與「城中村」結下了一世的緣分。

馬立安對城中村有著近乎執拗的熱愛。當聽到人們評價城中村「髒亂差、人口素質低」時，她便會忍不住為城中村「辯護」：「大城市裡，哪還能找到一個離市區二十分鐘路程的便宜地方？對於許多初來乍到的年輕人來說，他們奮鬥的起點便是城中村。」在她看來，城中村占深圳的總面積不超過百分之五，但卻住著超過一半的人口，城中村不僅讓來深圳的人立足，所提供的送水工、清潔工等基礎的職位，也讓進城的人們改變了生活和身分。那些來深圳尋夢的年輕人，如果不是「富二代」或者「官二代」，那麼初來乍到的他們，第一個落腳點便是城中村。這些人並不是素質低下的人，也不是拖累深圳發展的累贅，相反，他們是深圳的希望，而城中村，是他們夢開始的地方。如果沒有城中村裡便宜的房租、食物，那麼他們很可能沒法在這裡打拚。最終，這些年輕人憑藉自己努力走出城中村，走進城區，走進高樓大廈，成為一個體面的深圳人。馬立安住過田面、沙嘴、南頭老街的城中村，深感城中村為城市發展作出的貢獻，她決定將城中村作為一個社會話題來探索深圳。

「與其說這活力蘊藏在高級住宅區裡，不如說藏在像白石洲這樣的『城中村』中。因為高大上的地方不是成功的源泉，只是人們成功後享受的地方。而這些進了『城中村』的人，從『握手樓』中出來要扮演的是改變命運的角色。善待他們某種意義上來說就是保存了一個城市的活力。」馬立安不止一次表達過自己的觀點：沒有城中村的社會功能，就不會有深圳當今的發展速度和成果，更不會有支持這座城市的人才基礎。如何為這些人保留一塊「宿營地」就是她要探索的問題。

讓馬立安擔憂的是，當下的一些舊改項目，改造後就只有一個商場和高大上的住宅區。還有一些城中村，他們請了設計師做改造，變得比以前漂亮，但它的租金也不便宜了。如果城中村的租金都不便宜了，低收入者和年輕人該住在哪裡呢？這群人中絕大部分就必須生活在原經濟特區外，這意味著他們難以真正融入深圳。事實上，城中村為他們在這座城市擁有豐富的生活提供了可能性。二〇一三年，馬立安牽頭髮起組成了「城中村特工隊」公益組織，在深圳所有的城中村促進公共藝術，希望通過交流讓更多的人瞭解身邊的環境。二〇一四年初，白石洲村被列為深圳市舊改的最大片區。馬立安以項目策劃人身分，在白石洲組織了一個名為「握手302」的「小白鼠」式體驗項目，目的就是讓來自不同國度的藝術家、好奇人士體驗在深圳最大城中村的生活。通過文化、藝術來討論、關注城中村現象，傾聽對於城中村的不同的意見，與城中村的居民一起互動。他們在白石洲的握手樓裡租了一個小房間，不定期地策劃一些好玩的活動。例如，她曾做過一個名為「算數」的小活動，在牆上釘一排架子，用幾組光管拼成數字，兩邊分別以薪水、消費陳列，中間是每個月可以留下的存款，通過這種形式，她希望表達出年輕人選擇「城中村」的原因。馬立安和她的夥伴想通過「白鼠計畫」，讓外面的人入住白石洲，一來可以給他們一些不一樣的啟發；二來可以讓外來的人對城中村以及城中村改造有不一樣的感受。

馬立安對城中村的熱愛，很大程度上是由於和諧熱絡的鄰里關系。小孩是活躍白石洲社區關係的潤滑劑。這裡的小孩大都在附近的小學寄讀，下課後父母還未下班，他們便滿大街追逐嬉戲，碰上陌生人也不慌張，張著好奇的眼睛上下打量，甚至還湊上前去問東問西。一來二去，小孩已能和陌生人對上話。漸漸的，在小孩的帶動下，大人也開始互相熟絡起來。每週六，握手 302 舉行活動的時候，隔壁的鄰居都會主動幫忙，在寒冷的冬天，女主人還時常端來熱騰騰的潮州粥品與她分享。女主人的孩子們每次見到馬立安，都會主動用英語、中文問候她。這種和諧、融洽的鄰里關係，在所謂的成熟社區並不多見，從小就熱情、禮貌的孩子在城中村中反而更常見。而這些是在數百米之遙的華僑城裡感受不到的。在馬立安看來，這些就是城中村的「正能量」。

來深圳二十二年，馬立安常常會被問：「為什麼你會在中國待這麼久？」「美國人不會問這樣的問題，但中國人會。」她覺得這樣的差異很有意思。馬立安的丈夫楊阡，是她口中「最有趣的」胖鳥劇團創始人。「我的丈夫是我留在深圳的一個原因，還有一個是──因為中國這麼重要，深圳改變了世界這麼多。」馬立安說。

柯拜：當「倒爺」
賺個盆滿缽滿

　　一八四五年，英國商人柯拜在廣州黃埔長洲島建立柯拜船塢，這是外資在廣州建立的第一個大型工業企業，也是外資在我國興辦的第一個企業。柯拜船塢位於黃埔長洲島北部，現黃埔造船廠內。船塢是用老闆一約翰・柯拜（J. Couper）的名字命名的。一八四五年，大英輪船公司職員約翰・柯拜(蘇格蘭人)受公司派遣，任公司駐黃埔的代表，負責公司送入黃埔船隻的監修工作。柯拜到黃埔後，從當地的中國人手裡租了幾個泥船塢，僱用一批中國人從事修船業，很快便由一個監修變成一個工業資本家。為了擴大經營，他將船塢擴建為石船塢，後人稱之為「柯拜船塢」。這是外國人在中國開設的第一個造船塢，也是中國近代造船工業的開端。

　　一九七八年廣東率先進行價格「闖關」。「三來一補」外貿形式首度出現。一九七九年蛇口建立我國內地第一個出口加工區。中國經濟重入世界經濟大門。一九九〇年代中期，被簡稱為「廣交會」的中國進出口商品交易會吸引了大批外國人前來從事商貿活動。最早到來的是阿拉伯人，之後才是非洲人。他們發現與香港相比，廣州更適合居住、做生意。由於鏈式效應，越來越多的非洲人來到這裡「淘金」。「東西南北中，發財到廣東」，這句在二十世紀八〇年代傳遍中國大江南北，在今天對許多老外而言，同樣適用。在外國人眼裡，廣州給他們留下的最深刻印象並非「食在廣州」，而是到廣州經商做生意。由廣州市社科院發布的《2014 廣州城市國際化發展報告》關於廣州城市國際形象調查分析顯示，受訪在穗外國人對廣州「商貿經濟」印象最為深刻，有 58.6%的受訪者選擇了此項，認為廣州商業發達，機會多；只有35.9%的受訪者選擇了「特色飲食」為印象最為深刻。

近年來，在匯美服裝城和凱榮都商城做外貿生意的老闆們，切切實實地感受到了「國際競爭」的壓力——不僅要和國內同行競爭，還要和老外們搶生意。來自東北的張老闆就遭遇過幾次。「老外到我們店裡來買東西，我店鋪的小妹就用英語跟他談，這個時候就有個外國人進來跟他們說話，聊著聊著客人就跟著走了。剛開始小妹們還以為他們認識，但後來發覺不對勁，每次一有老外進來買東西，老是有人跟進來然後把他們拉走。後來才發現是這些人把客人拉到樓上去了」。

匯美商城八樓到十一樓，都是老外們的「地盤」，電梯裡張貼著寫滿外文的服裝廣告。過去，這些外國人都是中國老闆們的「客人」，過去從事的是「代購」的角色。從二〇〇八年開始，部分外籍商人開始逐步滲透進外貿的各個環節，繞過了中國批發商，直接跟廠裡打交道。「他們原來通過參加廣交會，結識不少中國製衣公司，一來二往彼此都相當熟悉。這些年他們就直接從廠裡拿貨到站西路這些商圈來做批發和零售。」老張說。從當初「代購」到現在自己「開淘寶」，從「後廠」逐步侵入到「前店」，他們僅僅用了兩三年的時間就在站西商圈形成規模並穩定下來。來自南非的 Sean，把廣州形容為「什麼都有的大金礦」，在廣州經營四年中非婚紗貿易後，他已經在開普敦買了一幢別墅和車子。「婚紗最貴的一條，在廣州的進貨價格是一千二百元人民幣，回到開普敦，婚紗很快就賣出去了，折合人民幣至少要五千元。」Sean 他們的生意不僅限於婚紗，還涉及鞋子、衣服、皮包。在他們眼中，廣州人也是很幸福的人，因為還有這麼多的批發市場讓老廣們「淘金」。

在廣州「小北—登峰—環市中路」一帶，非洲人聚居的現象已超過十年，外界冠之以「巧克力城」的稱號。在登峰街，有廣州街坊打趣：「老外的香水味我都聞習慣了。」登峰街揚名海外，在非洲人心目中有著特殊的地位。來自肯尼亞的 Albert 在廣州的第一張照片，便是在登峰街越洋商貿城門口拍下的。不是地標廣州塔，也不是千年古道北京路，而是登峰街，這裡才是他們心目中廣州的標志，足以向父老鄉親證明「是的，我來過廣州」。

來自馬里的阿龍，在中國奮鬥了十四年，已經能說一口流利的中文。年輕時，阿龍在馬里本地也是做點小生意，進貨渠道多為東南亞。二〇〇二年，奔著新開的批發市場有便宜貨源，抱著哪裡有錢賺就往哪奔赴的阿龍，跟著朋友就來到廣州闖蕩。讓他喜出望外的是，沒過多久，他就在這裡拼出了一片天地。「我剛來廣州的時候，在這裡拿貨的非洲人沒有現在多。儘管語言不同，但一做起生意來，跟中國批發商溝通卻很順暢。」阿龍說。從廣州起步的他，慢慢的，貨源擴大到青島、福州、佛山、東莞……他一般會挑選一些中意的服裝樣式，然後從各地的工廠訂貨，等到中國農曆新年時就回國進行售賣。只是，阿龍生意的巔峰時期已過。非洲的經濟不好，本國生意越來越難做，從中國進的貨存在賣不出去的風險。儘管如此，阿龍並不打算離開。「相比我們國家，中國還是遍地機會的，而且非洲經濟也會慢慢復甦，我已經習慣在這裡打拚了。」阿龍說。

藍龍：國際創客安營紮寨

二〇一三年九月十五日，是以色列人藍龍來到深圳的第一天。「哇哦，太神奇了，好多樹木啊，到處都是綠的！」在前往深圳市區的路上，看著窗外一片鬱鬱蔥蔥的景象，藍龍抑制不住內心的喜悅，興奮地對坐在身邊的司機師傅說。生機勃勃，是這種年輕的城市給藍龍的第一印象：有創新、有希望、有未來。此前，藍龍在上海待了三年，後被「挖」到深圳，擔任一家白酒公司的品牌開發與營銷總監。在百度上輸入「藍龍以色列」，能看不少藍龍寫的文章：《猶太人成功致富的九大秘訣》《可不可以不成功？猶太 80 後 RAFA 探索特別的創業文化》《以色列創業者 Rafa 說「猶太式教育」中的父親》等一系列文章，讓他被中國朋友稱為「猶太雞湯小王子」。來到深圳，一直是藍龍認為的最正確的選擇。

來深圳之前，藍龍對這座城市並沒有什麼概念。他在上海待了三年，有些厭倦了，決定來深圳完全是出於對新鮮事物的好奇和接受挑戰的興趣，對於這座城市沒有什麼期待，只知道它離香港很近，是一座海濱城市，有很多工廠和企業，僅此而已。在此創業居住了三年多，他將深圳看成了「大驚喜」。他常常跟自己的以色列朋友介紹，深圳是一座未來之城，而他對深圳的喜愛、欣賞和信賴，源於這座城市與他的祖國——「創業的國度」以色列非常相似。在深圳，藍龍從來沒有感覺自己是一個「外人」，事業也是做得順風順水。最近半年，他發出去的名片不下四千張，學校、企業邀請他的演講將近二十場。在藍龍看來，深圳和以色列都是移民彙集的地方。所到之處，不管是辦公室同事、咖啡館服務員或是在酒吧遇到的姑娘，碰到一個土生土長的本地人的幾率是極低的。這些移民成為了創新的引擎，因為創新就像是連接兩個不同的點，然後創造出一個全新的點。深圳的未來就如同今天的以色列，幾乎所有孩子的父母都來自於兩個完全不同的地方，而中國每座城市都有其獨特的文化和習俗，所以會帶來不同的觀念和想法。如今的藍龍，不僅經常在微信朋友圈裡發關於創新、創業的內容，還創辦了一家諮詢公司，為想要去以色列考察、投資的中國人以及希望到中國尋找合作機會的以色列人提供服務。在中國生活了六年多，他已經成為了「中國通」，對中國、對他所處的深圳的發展，也有了自己看法。「深圳經歷了三十八年的發展變化，從當初的三十萬人口到如今的一千五百萬人口，當時一無所知的漁民變成了如今掌握新技術的年輕人。一九七九年前的中國是比較封閉的，改革開放後中國正式向西方敞開大門，經歷了三十八年的高速發展。到今天變化仍然在發生，中國正在從過去的廉價出口向未來的有價值創新過渡。中國決心要從『全球製造大國』變成『全球創新大國』。這個願景真的能實現嗎？雖然目前還需等待觀望，但從政府的大力支持和民眾的高漲熱情來看，我相信，中國人民的『中國夢』終將會成為現實。」藍龍說。

對於不少來自美國硅谷的極客來說，「Shenzhen」並不是一個陌生的字眼。在這個面積差一點到二千平方公里的地方，聚集了不少的科技創新創業園。在不少外媒的報導中，深圳作為「China's Silicon Valley」（中國硅谷）被反覆提起，這是他們接觸中國的第一站。有人做出這樣的比喻，硅谷更像是一個發動機，在這裡你能嗅到前沿科技和未來趨勢；深圳則是能把這種動力應用到各種商業領域、發揚光大的地方。過去乃至現在，每當硅谷有新的變化時，深圳的創業者總是最先觀察到，模仿、拷貝，並且創造出新的機遇。誕生於深圳的互聯網巨頭騰訊，便是其中的佼佼者。騰訊早期最重要的產品 OICQ，是仿效由以色列青年維斯格、瓦迪和高德芬格開發的一款在互聯網上能夠快速直接交流的軟件 ICQ。一九九八年，騰訊正式開始了對 OICQ 的開發。在對 ICQ 的模仿的基礎上，騰訊進行了微創新：它把信息留存從客戶端轉移到服務器端，適應了當時中國的上網環境，還先後發明了斷點傳輸、群聊、截圖等功能。後來騰訊多項重大產品的開發，也都體現了這一特點。有人曾經總結：「騰訊十五年發展史，就是靠微創新幹死一個又一個競爭對手的商戰史。」

　　二〇一五年，加拿大創客傑瑟斯登陸深圳，成為國際創客中的一員，他參加的項目叫 HAX 的「硬件加速器」，總部位於舊金山，而在中國的「加速器」設在華強北，主要孵化硬件企業。法國人 Homeric 到深圳多年，曾經是某大公司的高端獵頭。因為思念家人，現有的聊天軟件又無法滿足他的需求，於是，在二〇一四年十二月，他辭職與兩個朋友一起創業，做 Shosha App。這款軟件會給「主人」每天發送一次拍攝「邀請」，一般每次拍攝五秒，在 Homeric 看來，就是這樣不經意的「記錄」，才能展現拍攝人真正的生活，而不是去擺拍或者炫耀，家人最需要看到的也是這些。說到深圳華強北，傑瑟斯連呼「太神奇」。「走到樓下，就能買到硬件創新和設計所需的各種元器件，價格還不到北美的三分之一。甚至有時候不用走出辦公室，賣家就把我需要的元器件送了上來。」

事實上，剛到深圳的創客們基本都有這樣的一種印象：方便。這種方便可能體現在硬件的採購流程上，也可能體現在銷售的渠道上。來自法國的 Christophe 與傑瑟斯有著近乎一致的感覺：「硬件的採購流程，一般在美國或者歐洲，這可能需要好幾天甚至幾週，而對於一個創業公司來說，時間是一個不小的成本。」

距離深圳七十餘公里的東莞，是世界聞名的「世界工廠」。一九七八年九月，一家港資企業太平手袋廠在東莞建廠，成為全國第一家「三來一補」企業，這標誌著東莞農村工業化就此起步。中國經濟從此與世界有了割不斷的臍帶。隨著東莞加工貿易的壯大，人們一度用「東莞塞車，全球缺貨」來形容東莞製造業的重要地位。近年來，由於長期快速發展積累的深層次矛盾，加上國際金融危機的沖擊，以及中國經濟發展進入新常態，東莞遭遇了「成長的煩惱」，面臨「雙重擠壓」。在新一輪的產業轉型升級中，東莞搖身一變，從「世界工廠」成為「創業沃土」，尤其是高新技術企業，如同雨後春筍般冒出。在這其中，就有意大利人 Agostino 創辦的一家環保科技公司。Agostino 的公司專業從事軟化水、純水、污水處理技術開發與應用，在環保越來越受到重視的今天，銷售額已經突破了億元。Agostino 的東莞的經歷，是這座城市成長軌跡的縮影。二〇〇六年，Agostino 陪同父母來莞打理一個家具廠，這是他第一次來莞。然而，在二〇〇八年，受國際金融危機影響，當年倚重外貿出口的東莞製造業遭遇寒流，東莞八百五十七家外企關停外遷。Agostino 的父母也在不久後將家具廠轉讓並回國。然而，Agostino 卻不願意走了。在這裡，他有了心愛的姑娘，「美得像公主一樣」的陝西姑娘賀江燕。Agostino 留了下來，並另闢蹊徑，決定運營一家科技環保有限公司。

「騰籠換鳥」，讓企業轉型升級，是東莞應對危機的一項重要舉措。東莞一位官員稱，改革開放以來，東莞一直是以外貿加工型經濟為主，也以此奠定「世界加工廠」的地位，但東莞這些企業多數屬於代工生產或者貼牌生產，自主品牌並不多，高附加值和豐厚利潤都被品牌商拿走，剩下的就是代工廠微薄的人工利潤。而「騰籠換鳥」，即是把現有的傳統製造業從目前的產業基地「轉移出去」，再把「先進生產力」轉移進來，以達到經濟轉型、產業升級的目的。Agostino 的決定無疑契合了這一舉措。Agostino 與太太「強強聯合」——Agostino 主攻採購和技術，賀江燕則主要負責政府和企業方面的銷售。除了研發和銷售環保設備外，Agostino 並沒有完全丟掉老本行，他的公司還經營家具雕刻設備、真空包裝設備。二〇〇六年，Agostino 從意大利引進國際頂尖的專業木工雕刻機械，可用在雕塑和裝飾品生產領域。二〇〇八年，又從意大利引進奧維德真空包裝機和包裝袋，成為該品牌亞洲區的總代理。Agostino一直很慶幸做出留下的決定，如今的他，財務自由，生活美滿。在東莞十年，他已經習慣了每個週末的早晨與太太和女兒一起出來喝早茶，到公園裡溜躂溜躂，看看晨練的人們，感受這座熱火朝天、飛速發展的城市背後的歲月靜好。

昌明文庫‧悅讀中國　A0607036

中國夢‧廣東故事——開放的廣東

作　　　者	劉曉星
版權策畫	李煥芹
責任編輯	呂玉姍

發 行 人	陳滿銘
總 經 理	梁錦興
總 編 輯	陳滿銘
副總編輯	張晏瑞
編 輯 所	萬卷樓圖書股份有限公司
排　　　版	菩薩蠻數位文化有限公司
印　　　刷	維中科技公司
封面設計	菩薩蠻數位文化有限公司

出　　　版　昌明文化有限公司

桃園市龜山區中原街 32 號

電話　(02)23216565

發　　　行　萬卷樓圖書股份有限公司

臺北市羅斯福路二段 41 號 6 樓之 3

電話　(02)23216565

傳真　(02)23218698

電郵　SERVICE@WANJUAN.COM.TW

大陸經銷

廈門外圖臺灣書店有限公司

　　電郵　JKB188@188.COM

ISBN 978-986-496-400-0

2019 年 3 月初版

定價：新臺幣 300 元

如何購買本書：

1. 轉帳購書，請透過以下帳戶

　合作金庫銀行　古亭分行

　戶名：萬卷樓圖書股份有限公司

　帳號：0877717092596

2. 網路購書，請透過萬卷樓網站

　網址　WWW.WANJUAN.COM.TW

大量購書，請直接聯繫我們，將有專人為您

服務。客服：(02)23216565 分機 610

如有缺頁、破損或裝訂錯誤，請寄回更換

版權所有‧翻印必究

Copyright©2019y WanJuanLou Books CO., Ltd.

All Right Reserved　　　　　**Printed in Taiwan**

國家圖書館出版品預行編目資料

中國夢.廣東故事——開放的廣東 / 劉曉星
著.-- 初版.-- 桃園市：昌明文化出版；臺北
市：萬卷樓發行, 2019.03
　　冊；　公分
ISBN 978-986-496-400-0(平裝)

1.區域研究　2.廣東省

673.3　　　　　　　　　108002850